BERGOGLIO'S LIST

BERGOGLIO'S LIST

How a Young Francis Defied a Dictatorship and Saved Dozens of Lives

NELLO SCAVO

TRANSLATED BY BRET THOMAN

SAINT BENEDICT+PRESS

Charlotte, North Carolina

Originally published in Italian as *La Lista di Bergoglio* by Nello Scavo.

Copyright © 2013 Editrice Missionaria Italiana
Via di Corticella 179/4, 01428
Bolgona, Italy

English translation by Bret Thoman copyright © 2014 Saint Benedict Press.

Cover design by Caroline Kiser.

Typeset by Lapiz.

Front Cover: (Photo by Franco Origlia/Getty Images); Back Jacket: (Daniel Garcia/AFP/Getty Images); Front Flap: (Daniel Garcia/AFP/Getty Images).

ISBN: 978-1-61890-626-7

Published in the United States by
Saint Benedict Press
PO Box 410487
Charlotte, NC 28241
www.SaintBenedictPress.com

Printed and bound in the United States of America

To Stella and Pietro

Love truth, show yourself as you are,
without pretense and without fear and without concern.
And if the truth costs you persecution, accept it;
and if torment, bear it. And if for the truth
you had to sacrifice yourself and your life,
be strong in your sacrifice.
(Giuseppe Moscati)

To Fathers Filippo and Silvio Alaimo,
My Jesuits

CONTENTS

PART ONE
THE REASON FOR INQUIRY

PART TWO
THE STORIES

PART THREE
ANSWERS FOUND

PREFACE

A T this writing, summer of 2014, two generations have grown up without having lived through Argentina's "Dirty War," which pitted a far-right-wing military dictatorship or "junta" against anyone considered subversive. The "subversives" targeted by the junta ranged from genuine Marxist guerillas, to members of trade unions, to Catholic "church ladies" who dared petition the government to reveal the fates of family members who had been arrested and then just disappeared.

To this day there is no accurate count of how many people fell victim to the regime. A rough calculation is 19,000 shot down in the streets, 30,000 "disappeared" and presumed dead (among them approximately 500 children), untold thousands imprisoned, and perhaps as many as two million Argentinians who went into exile.

At the same time, there is no accurate count of how many escaped thanks to the courage of men and women who risked their own lives to save others, sometimes complete strangers. Their heroism recalls the men and women in Nazi-occupied Europe during World War II who saved the lives of countless Jews, Slavs, Russians, Gypsies, and other targets of the Third Reich.

The title of this book is inspired by one of the most celebrated saviors of World War II, Oskar Schindler, the subject of Thomas Keneally's book and Steven Spielberg's film of the same name, *Schindler's List*.

When the war began, Schindler was no saint. He was a chronic womanizer who cheated on his wife and a war profiteer who cultivated friendships with Nazi generals and concentration camp commandants. Yet at some point, through the mysterious workings of Almighty God, his long-dormant Catholic conscience woke up. He then made it his personal responsibility to save the lives of approximately 1000 Jewish men, women, and children.

Bergoglio's List is the story of how then Father Jorge Mario Bergoglio—now Pope Francis—risked his life to save approximately 100 people who had been identified as "enemies" of the Argentinian junta. It appears there were dozens more whom he was able to warn before the authorities could come to arrest them.

It takes incredible courage to stand up to evil on a grand scale, and that is what the military junta was. In 1976 the armed forces launched a *coup d'etat* that toppled the government of President Perón. The junta drove out of office governors and judges across Argentina; dissolved congress and the supreme court; abolished the constitution; banned labor unions; censored newspapers and other media outlets; and outlawed all forms of political dissent.

The viciousness of the junta's campaign against its

opponents is difficult to comprehend. The junta created a climate of terror in which people were picked up on the streets and dragged away to detention centers. There they were brutally tortured to extract confessions and forced to incriminate others. Then so often these prisoners simply "disappeared." Many were shot and dumped into unmarked graves. Others were thrown from helicopters while still alive into the open ocean, their bodies never to be found again.

Father Bergoglio, at the time superior of the Jesuits in Argentina, detested the viciousness of the regime. He began helping anyone who appealed to him for protection. One of the people on "the List" is Gonzalo Mosca, a left-wing labor organizer who was staunchly anti-clerical. He had hoped he could lose himself in the vast suburbs of Buenos Aires, but the military hunted him down. When the caretaker of his apartment building warned him that the military was closing in and ready to kill him, Mosca turned to the only person he felt he could trust, his brother, who was a Jesuit priest.

Father Mosca said he thought he had a solution. He called his philosophy professor from his days in the seminary, Father Bergoglio. At a predetermined location, Bergoglio picked up Mosca and drove him to the Jesuit College of San Miguel. There he was hidden for four days while Bergoglio organized an escape route that called for a brief air flight, a boat trip into Brazil, a stay with the Brazilian Jesuits, and finally a flight to Europe and safety. Recalling what Bergoglio did for him, Mosca has said, "I don't know of other people who would have done the same thing. I don't know if anyone else would have saved me without knowing me at all."

Alicia Oliveira was Argentina's first female criminal court judge. The junta forced her from office, and then began to hound her. This mother of three young children suddenly found herself on the run, unable to visit her family, unable to console her terrified children. Father Bergoglio arranged meetings between Oliveira and her children in a disused corridor of the College of San Miguel. As the situation became increasingly dangerous for her, Bergoglio found a unique way out of the country for Oliveira and several other victims—in the cargo hold of a commercial vessel carrying fruit to Uruguay.

After the junta had collapsed, former members of the regime and some of their sympathizers tried to destroy Father Bergoglio's reputation by suggesting he had been a double agent, occasionally smuggling out of the country people wanted by the regime, but more often cooperating with the regime in its round up of priests, intellectuals, and others who opposed the junta. St. John Paul II experienced a similar detraction campaign in his native Poland under the Communists. Publically tarring the reputation of political opponents is a common practice of corrupt regimes, including the former Soviet Empire.

Prominent Argentinians, themselves victims of the regime, have come forward to defend Bergoglio. Adolfo Maria Pérez Esquivel, a civil rights activist who had been active in opposing the junta and later won the Nobel Peace Prize, has stated categorically, "There were clergymen who were accomplices of the dictatorship [but] Bergoglio was not one of them." Graciela Fernandez Meijide, who served on the National Commission to investigate the fate of the disappeared, concurs with Pérez Esquivel, "There is no evidence that Bergoglio collaborated with the dictatorship. I know this personally." Once something wicked, however untrue, has been published about a prominent figure, it is difficult to convince the public that the charge is a lie. Yet the testimony of such renowned targets of the dictatorship as Pérez Esquivel and Fernandez Meijide goes a long way to dispel the "black legend" of Bergoglio the clandestine collaborator.

In this volume, author Nello Scavo has collected wonderful, inspiring stories of Father Bergoglio's courage, the gratitude of the people he helped, and their astonishment, even all these years later, that he ran such dangerous risks for their sakes. I don't want to steal any more of Scavo's thunder, so I'll stop summarizing these stories here so that you, the reader, can enjoy them as I have.

Since his election to the papacy on March 13, 2013, Jorge Maria Bergoglio—Pope Francis—has been celebrated in the media for the simplicity of his way of life, for his down-to-earth manner with all types of people, for his eagerness to see what is best even in Catholics who perhaps are not living the faith as fully as one would hope, and for his off-the-cuff style of speaking (which, to be honest, has sometimes led to some confusion among the Catholic faithful). This media coverage could give the impression that Francis is a "soft" pope, what used to be called touchy-feely. But that is one reason why the eyewitness accounts in this book are so important: they reveal to us another side of Pope Francis—as a man of tremendous courage and moral certainty, who was willing to lay down his life to save victims of a savage regime.

Thomas J. Craughwell
August 15, 2014
The Feast of the Assumption of Our Lady

Thomas J. Craughwell is the author of more than two dozen books, including *Pope Francis: The Pope from the End of the Earth* from Saint Benedict Press.

PART ONE

THE REASON
FOR INQUIRY

CHAPTER 1

DOZENS OF PEOPLE ON THAT "LIST"

HE appeared unexpectedly on their television screen in a live broadcast transmitted around the world. There, up upon a monumental balcony, the man to whom they owed their life gazed over an incredulous crowd. It was as if they had regained their sight after having a cataract removed. Some of them had not seen him since that day of farewell long ago when they had set out adventurously towards Europe, or sought shelter across the border, or even hid in the trunk of his car while he defied the military curfew. For four decades, they had struggled to try to find a way to remember without suffering any longer. Few succeeded.

He was dressed in white. He said his name was Francis. "Bergoglio saved many of them—more than even he himself can remember," an old friend confided to me a few hours later. The time for forgetting was now over.

3

Instead, now was the time for inquiry. First I would go to Buenos Aires. Then, I would follow the road to their salvation which led to Uruguay and Paraguay. From there my search would continue. I would discover people who had been saved from sure execution: the communist unionist, the former catechist, the university teacher, the judge, the atheist journalist, the political activist, the Marxist theologian, and the bride and groom persecuted because they preferred a life among the poor instead of one of ease. Some still live in Argentina, but many have never stopped feeling in exile.

Yet no one, beginning with his closest friends—far from limited to a few trusted people—absolutely nobody wanted to help send me down the right path. Neither his nephew, the Jesuit priest Fr. José Luis Narvaja, who leads the Thomas Falkner institute in Buenos Aires. Nor Alicia Oliveira, a judge and lawyer whom Bergoglio protected on numerous occasions. Nor Father Juan Carlos Scannone, considered the greatest living theologian in Argentina, who shared with me the story how he, too, escaped persecution.

"Sorry, now it's up to you to discover the rest of the story." He had a curious demeanor, as if he was hiding something. Was this conspiracy of silence an effort to protect Pope Francis's public image? No names. Not even a trace or a morsel of truth that would lead to Fr. Jorge's "list." "I'm sure you can understand," they responded to my persistence.

Slowly, the "list" began to come together: names, confirmations, testimonies of bravery and secret agent shrewdness. As it did, the answer to a question that had obsessed me began to take shape: "Why did Fr. Jorge's friends wish to remain silent when they should have cared deeply about divulging such amazing truth?"

From the wisdom of his eighty-one years, Fr. Scannone limits himself to a mere "*Sì*" in response to a logical theory that all of a sudden flashed through my mind. But to my mind as a reporter—very different from the less impulsive logic of an historian—it made no sense.

I posed this question to him at the end of a long conversation in a secluded room in the College of San Miguel*—the headquarters of Bergoglio's daring clandestine operations. We spoke about unhealed wounds. Of mothers who each week still walk toward the Plaza de Mayo, in a melancholic Via Crucis-like procession. And of grandmothers who know children who were born in the filthy corridors of detention centers and were soon adopted by regime families while their birth parents were killed. We spoke of an entire generation archived in thirteen letters: *desaparecidos* (the Spanish term for those who disappeared or went missing in Argentina during the Dirty War†).

---

* San Miguel is a municipality within Greater Buenos Aires, approximately 30 kilometers (18 miles) from the capital's city center. The *Colegio Máximo* and the *Universidad del Salvador*—frequently mentioned in this book—are in San Miguel.

† Dirty War: (Spanish: Guerra Sucia) is the name used to describe the "war" waged by the military and security forces of the Argentine government against left-wing guerrillas, political dissidents, and those accused of socialism or communism.

The wearied "yes" spoken by the elderly Jesuit theologian was his response to the following question: "Do the pope's friends remain silent so that they will not be seen as substantiating the suspicion that Bergoglio is trying to use them to manipulate the events during the dictatorship years towards his favor?"

Moreover, for thirty years the provincial of the Jesuits himself (later auxiliary bishop and finally archbishop of Buenos Aires and primate of Argentina) chose silence. This also shows the way Pope Francis understands freedom and safeguards it for himself and desires it for others: to the point of experiencing personal loss.

Yet, I am grateful for that silence. Because what follows is the fruit of laborious research, the reconstruction of the stories of people saved by Bergoglio. The "list" remains largely incomplete. Most of the would-be *desaparecidos* have built a life for themselves as normal as possible. They have kept evil outside their door. Yet, every now and then, it comes back and knocks. As in group therapy or twelve-step meetings, they try to live their lives one day at a time. For decades now they have tried to fill the emptiness created by the insanity of that period with goodness. Some are grateful they can still witness the sun rising in the morning. Yet others are wracked with survivors' guilt for not ending up like the others—at the bottom of the Atlantic.

For a long time, some have accused him [Bergoglio] of having turned away, of being a coward, or even an accomplice to the regime. But the people on the "list"—those who speak from these pages through personal encounters, interviews, investigative documents, and statements made during inquiry commissions—testify for him. Some of those "saved by Bergoglio" have asked me not to mention where or how our meetings took place. Others preferred to refer me back to newspaper clippings and written submissions, which I combined with the findings noted in court documents. For reasons of confidentiality (that the reader can understand given the sensitivity of the topic), I have sometimes edited out of my reconstructions and certain methods, places, and dates.

And yes, there is reason to tell the story of an unknown Bergoglio: of his courage during those nights unphased by the military raids; of the days spent passing back and forth between his prayer breviary and their roadblocks; of strategizing ways to avoid the checkpoints; of sidetracking police and outmaneuvering generals; of leading young men destined for the clandestine slaughterhouses safely across the border. Some call them "gestures." Others—in more evangelical language—"good works."

A question remains, however, without a definitive answer. How many were there? Fr. Miguel Civita, someone on the "list," confirms having seen Bergoglio help many people "leave the country." And those he helped were not limited to priests or seminarians. Fr. Civita said, "At the *Colegio Máximo* different people came in alone or in small groups for a spiritual retreat. They stayed a few days and then left. But the exercises should have lasted for a week." I knew he was referring to dissident lay people whom Father Jorge helped escape. But how? "By any means and always at the risk of very much."

Each person protected by Bergoglio says he personally assisted in the rescue of at least twenty additional people. The testimonies cover a wide period of time. To hazard a conservative estimate, it seems that Fr. Jorge brought more than one hundred people to safety. Dozens more, as we shall see, were consequentially saved "preventively"; that is, warned by the future pope before they were ever abducted. And we can add still more people who were saved from the regime without their knowledge due to the maneuvers of Fr. Jorge, as some of the stories in this book will tell, "by thus averting new arrests. During interrogations conducted under torture, other names could have come out. Names that now would be counted among the missing on the list of the *desaparecidos.*"

I sincerely hope it is not offensive to the person concerned, but it seems that Bergoglio's "list" is really longer and includes "more people than even he himself can remember."

CHAPTER 2

ARGENTINA UNDER THE HEEL OF THE MILITARY

ARGENTINA'S Armed Forces led a coup d'état on March 24, 1976. Under the pretext of launching the "National Reorganization Process,"* the military junta deposed President Isabelita Perón (who had succeeded her husband, Juan) as well as governors and deputy governors. Further, they dissolved Congress and removed each and every member of the Supreme Court. The military won the war but did not seek peace. Instead, they took control of the state by abolishing constitutional rights, suspending political activity and the right to associate, prohibiting unions, overseeing newspapers, and abducting political militants, social activists, and guerrillas. They created a climate of

---

*   The National Reorganization Process (Spanish: *Proceso de Reorganización Nacional*), was the term used by the military dictatorship that ruled Argentina from 1976 to 1983 implying their effort to restore order and subdue the country's violent political situation.

9

terror through systematic mass disappearances as well torturing those they arrested to extract information. In a further grotesque violation of human rights, newborn infants
delivered by inmates in clandestine detention centers were
sequestered and, in turn, given in adoption to families connected to the regime.

The military junta was a triumvirate led by commanders of the three military branches: General Videla of the
Army, Admiral Emilio Massera of the Navy, and Brigadier
General Orlando Ramón Agosti of the Air Force. The military leaders took upon themselves the right to appoint the
country's president from among retired officers. They were
to be members of the CAL (*Comisión de Asesoramiento
Legislativo*) in accordance with the rule of the so-called
"fourth man," which was supposed to ensure separation
between the military and the government.

But in reality it was nothing more than a ploy so that
even the most reluctant players in the international community would view the coup that claimed "Argentine
uniqueness" as legitimate when compared to the bru-
talities taking place in neighboring countries. General
Videla immediately assumed the presidency until he
was replaced by Viola in 1981, who was succeeded by
Galtieri, and then by Bignone in 1982. In an effort to hide
their real intentions, the conspirators would not tear up
the country's Constitution. Instead, they trampled on it.
In word, the foundational charter remained law, on one
condition: that it did not conflict with the provisions of
the Statute of the National Reorganization Process. This
was a contradiction which was not noticed at first.

All this took place due to the silence that had spread throughout the country, as if the years of insecurity had created an epidemic of mass speechlessness. Marzia Rosti, professor of Latin American history in the department of political science at the University of Milan, argues in his book, *Argentina*: "The military intervention of 1976 was desired, if not actually demanded, by at least part of the country's citizens. They hoped it would resolve the tensions and social conflicts that previous governments had failed to deal with. Although it was necessary to intervene vigorously, the military undoubtedly went far beyond what the people expected."

The clean-slate operation against the guerrillas generated results within just a few months. The dismemberment of social organizations led to the disappearance of at least 30,000 people, the appropriation of more than 500 children of those sentenced to death, the imprisonment of thousands of political activists, the exile of approximately two million people, and 19,000 victims shot dead in the street.

In 1983, the regime finally unraveled. Humiliated by defeat in their war effort to re-take the Falkland Islands from the United Kingdom, the generals were cornered both by national as well as international public opinion. On the domestic front, they were accused of having massacred hundreds of young militants, while abroad people were finally taking notice of the junta's true character and brutality.

And so began the first whispers of the existence of mass graves and cemeteries of nameless crosses. For the first time since the era of the *conquistadores,* another Spanish word originating in Latin America would once again darken the pages of history textbooks: *desaparecidos.* At first, there was talk of only a few hundred. But after investigations of the relatives of those who had "disappeared," a conservative estimate was revealed: 30,000 had been *chupados*—sucked up—into the void of absolute and ruthless power. From April to December of 1985, the trial of high-ranking military officers took place in the Federal Court of Buenos Aires in what was called the *juicio del siglo* (trial of the century) and in what should have accompanied the country's transition to democracy. For days, the entire subcontinent remained glued to newspapers, radios, and television sets. After a total of 900 hours of hearings, 833 witnesses, and tons of documents a sentence was finally announced on December 9, 1985.

Marzia Rosti recalls in *Argentina:*

> It was lighter both in terms of the prosecutors' demands and the expectations of public opinion. Only Videla and Massera were sentenced to life imprisonment. The majority of Argentinians believed that the two would serve their sentences, and they looked forward to the beginning of the trials of lower-ranking soldiers. But between 1987 and 1988, the prospect of thousands of new trials, in addition to publicizing the scope of the tragedy, created resistance and tension among lower-ranking

soldiers. They claimed they were merely acting in defense of the country [from domestic
terrorism]. The fear of a new coup put the
fragile democracy to the test and proved that
the Armed Forces, who had controlled state
institutions since 1930, had not gone away and
continued to arouse fear.

The world would have to wait almost until the turn
of the century for true justice to arrive in the *Cono Sur*
("the Southern Cone"—the region south of the Tropic of
Capricorn comprised of six Latin American countries:
Argentina, Falkland Islands, Chile, Uruguay, Paraguay,
and Brazil). Yet even today, many trials are still ongoing.

The "passion according to Captain Astiz"

Christians not "in line" with the government automati-
cally found themselves in its crosshairs. The military
junta deployed its top men from the Secret Service to
paramilitary patrols against them. It is clear that Videla
and his men believed they would be able to count on the
church hierarchy for "sins of omission" or even outright
complicity. The story that will be told here—that of the
group from the parish of Santa Cruz, a beautiful parish
in Buenos Aires—shows well the climate and the dangers
that threatened communities of the Argentine church
both from within and from without. It is a terrible example of the risks faced personally by Bergoglio as well as
the risks of those he protected while he was provincial of
the Jesuits in his efforts to save lives from the repressive

government. This was a dark story—one of many—in the age of state terrorism that Cardinal Bergoglio would face in testimony given to Argentine judges in 2010 (published in the Appendix).

With devilish skill, a spy was able to gain the trust of family members of some *desaparecidos* who met in the parish of Santa Cruz. Looking like a "blonde angel," Gustavo Niño was friendly with everyone. With blue eyes (rare in that area) and the face of a well-educated student, he grew up dividing his time between home and church. He used to recount the story of how his brother had become a *chupado* by some government assassin.

The handsome Gustavo was affectionately referred to as *El Rubito* (the blond guy) around the parish. It was not uncommon for Niño to stop and chat with some of the moms in the churchyard or with the nuns in the garden next to the church. They would talk about their fears and concerns for the fate of the *desaparecidos*, as well as their aversion to the junta soldiers. Before going home, *el Rubito* would encourage them to be strong. He would say good-bye, embrace them warmly, and give them a peck on the cheek.

A long time later, the parishioners of Santa Cruz would discover the other side of the Rubito. His was not a kiss of compassion; it was the kiss of Judas—the agreed-upon signal to indicate whom the military intelligence agents should "target." Gustavo Niño's real name was Alfredo Astiz. In truth, he was an Argentine navy officer. His victims included: two French nuns, Léonie Duquet and Alice Dumont, a crime for which Astiz was sentenced in Paris;

one of the founders of the Mothers of Plaza de Mayo*, Azucena Villaflor; and journalist and writer, Rodolfo Walsh, one of the most articulate minds to denounce the senselessness of the National Reorganization Process. The former frigate captain once created a circus act by provocatively appearing in court while reading a book titled, *Volver a matar* (*Return to Kill*). At the time of the dictatorship, his mission was to silence those in the church who had chosen not to genuflect to the generals' uniform. A few months after the coup of 1976, Astiz was able to infiltrate the group that met in the parish of Santa Cruz which the junta considered to be a den of subversives. Niño's signature even found its way onto a petition demanding the release of several political prisoners whose names had been published in the newspaper, *La Nación*, on December 10, 1977 by human rights organizations. Niño himself accompanied the activists to the meetings that were held in Santa Cruz, in the semi-central district of San Cristobal. They trusted the blond Gustavo to the point of assigning him scoutmaster of the boy scouts in the parish—a role he played with disingenuous skill.

The Court of Cassation in Rome effectively summarized his role as an "exterminating angel" in its statement during the Argentine officer's sentencing and conviction for the death of three Italian immigrants: "While exercising his role of command over NCOs and subordinates

---

* The Mothers of the Plaza de Mayo (Spanish: *Asociación Madres de Plaza de Mayo*) was an association of Argentine mothers whose children "disappeared" during the Dirty War.

while in direct collaboration with senior officers in the *Grupo de tareas 3.3.2* ("work groups" was the colloquial name for kidnapping teams within the Argentine military dictatorship), Officer Astiz acted with full knowledge of criminal complicity by maintaining and managing a clandestine prison where the three victims were held continuously during their captivity."

El Rubito described himself fairly accurately. This, too, was a trick he used to justify the crimes he committed, as if his training had disassociated him from his conscience. "I state that the Armada taught me how to destroy. They did not teach me how to build up; rather, they taught me how to tear down. I know how to use land mines and bombs, I know how to infiltrate, I know how to disarm an organization, and I know how to kill. I know how to do all of this very well. I do not deny that I am a brute. But I have made only one reasonable action in my life, which was to enlist in the Armada."

There is some truth in this. But in re-reading his words, it is not difficult to note the duplicity within Alfredo-Gustavo. It is as if the uniform stripped him of his humanity. Thus, he chose to go down in history as an automaton. But his strategy did not work. Despite protection, immunity laws (fortunately suppressed), and attempts at corrupting the trial, el Rubito was sentenced to life imprisonment by the Buenos Aires Tribunal.

The Italian court notes that

> the criminal detention facility counted among
> its institutional goals that of secretly removing

prisoners whom the guards did not believe would ever obey the dictatorial regime. This involved a significant number of prisoners determined to be twenty percent. The defendant, moreover, confided to a witness that executions (by throwing prisoners from aircraft flying at high altitudes over the Atlantic) were sometimes also utilized in order to free up space when there was not enough capacity to receive new prisoners.

On Christmas Eve of 1977, the junta decided that the "subversives" of Santa Cruz (mostly women) should be eliminated. They were considered bad examples to other Catholic communities; the fascism of Videla and his cohorts would not permit division. The double persona of Astiz-Niño had been around for too long. They were afraid he would be discovered at any moment, and activist groups around the country would then know that nowhere was safe from regime infiltration. It was time to act.

On January 26, 1977, he risked more than he should have. On a busy morning, the *Grupo de Tareas 3.3.2* arrested Norma Burgos, the wife of a senior *Montonero* leader.* Together with the team of soldiers he commanded, Astiz hid in Burgos' home. There they waited for María Berger, another *Montonera* leader, who was expected to arrive the next day.

---

* The *Montonero* movement was a Peronist socialist-inspired guerrilla organization operating in Argentina since the seventies. It was almost completely destroyed by the dictatorship.

At 8:30 a.m. Dagmar Hagelin, a seventeen-year-old Swedish girl who was a friend of Norma, stopped by her house to say hello. She was tall, blonde, and blue-eyed. The men in the *Grupo* thought she was Berger. As soon as she came into the yard, Astiz and his men jumped toward her with their weapons drawn. But Dagmar was a well-trained athlete, and she instinctively ran down the street as fast as she could. Astiz and a corporal named Peralta ran after her yelling at her to stop. They wanted her alive to interrogate her with their usual methods. Dagmar Hagelin ran even faster out of fear. She had nothing to hide, but she knew what would happen if she could not get away.

Dagmar made it a few yards, but the officers were armed. El Rubito slashed her in the head, and she fell down injured on the pavement. The soldiers stopped a taxi and threw the Swede in the trunk. Eyewitnesses later recounted that Dagmar Hagelin was bleeding, but was alive and conscious. With the little strength she had left, she tried to prevent them from closing the trunk. She was later seen alive in the ESMA detention center.* But after March of 1977, she was never heard from again.

Following that event, Astiz tried to stay out of sight. During Advent of 1977, the Grupo de Tareas 3.3.2 went to work against the parish of Santa Cruz. They abducted

---

* ESMA (Spanish acronym: *Escuela superior de mecánica de la Armada*) was the Navy School of Mechanics in Buenos Aires used as a clandestine prison of detention and torture during the period of the dictatorship. It was the most notorious one during the Dirty War, and is frequently referred to in this book.

the whole "gang": Azucena Villaflor, Esther Ballestrino, and María Ponce (the three founders of the Mothers of Plaza de Mayo), the French nuns Alice Dumont and Léonie Duquet, and human rights activists Angela Auad, Remo Berardo, Horacio Elbert, José Fondevilla, Eduardo Horane, Raquel Bulit, and Patricia Oviedo.

Between December 8 and December 10, 1977 about ten people connected to the *Madres de Plaza de Mayo* were "sucked up." Azucena Villaflor was dragged away as she hurried to the newsstand to buy an edition of the *Nación* newspaper. That day it had published an appeal to the authorities: "*Por una Navidad en paz solo pedimos verdad*" ("For a Christmas in peace, we ask only for truth").

During that operation, Astiz continued to play his false role in the community, as he embraced and kissed "subversives" who had escaped the first raid. Then, suddenly, he went silent and was not heard from again. The serpent was successful in his task—so much that the name of Gustavo Niño was counted among the list of *desaparecidos* for years.

Lisandro Raúl Cubas, a former inmate in the clandestine prison of ESMA, later told the CONADEP* that "even in her worst moments of pain, Sister Alice [Dumont], who was isolated in a *capucha* [a kind of dark, windowless cage in which prisoners of ESMA were segregated]

---

* National Commission on the Disappearance of Persons (Spanish: *Comisión Nacional sobre la Desaparición de Personas*, CONADEP) was an organization in Argentina created in 1983 to investigate the fate of the *desaparecidos* during the era of the Dirty War.

wanted to know about the fate of her companions. And in full irony, she wanted to know in particular about the blond guy, who turned out to be none other than the frigate captain, Astiz."

Apparently, the entire group of Santa Cruz was killed off. After a grizzly assortment of tortures, the victims were finally eliminated in a death flight [over the ocean]. At the end of 1977, several bodies were found along a beach and buried hastily with the words *N.N.* in the cemetery of General Lavalle—300 kilometers (186 miles) south of Buenos Aires in a remote clearing inland from the Bay of Samborombón. Years later, five victims were identified and their remains were transferred to the cemetery in the church yard [of Santa Cruz].

Life as a "*chupado*" (sucked up)

At the time of the dictatorship, "X96" was a technician who worked at the national atomic energy commission. Then, in 1977 he was abducted. The ESMA executioners tried to exploit his knowledge of physics to improve their torture methods. "X96" lived for four years *chupado* by the repressive government. He is one of the few who lived to tell what it was like to be desaparecido. His real name was Mario Villani.

"From the moment you were kidnapped, you became desaparecido; that is, you ceased to exist from one day to the next. You did not exist to your family, friends, or co-workers. I was arrested on the morning of November 18, 1977. I was imprisoned in five different clandestine detention centers: Club Atlético, Banco, Olimpo, *División Cuatrerismo de Quilmes*, and ESMA," he recounted as a witness during the trial of General Guillermo Suárez Mason.

The normal sequence of events was: "*desaparición*, then torture, then death." The majority of desaparecidos spent entire days and nights hooded, shackled, and blind-folded in cells so small they were called a "tube." You then left the tube for a visit with the "surgeon." But this had nothing to do with health care; the "surgeon" was a tor-turer. When you left, the "operating room" [you] reeked of blood and disinfectant. Next, you ended up among the *trasladados* (the transferred). Finally you were liberated: the firing squad put an end to your suffering.

"In addition to physical tortures inflicted during interrogations, there was constant psychological tor-ture. Daily life," recalls Villani, "was extremely humili-ating. When you entered, they assigned you a code that we inmates had to use even among ourselves. Mine was X96." Villani continued:

> Towards the end of 1978, I was at the Garage Olimpo, [on] one of the occasions. I worked in the electronics workshop where they had me repair appliances, known as 'spoils of war,' that came in after the looting of prisoners' homes. When Suárez Mason entered the work-shop, he wanted to know two things. First, how to localize television interference which the *Montoneros* were doing. Next, he wanted

to know if I could produce similar interference. Although the solution was fairly simple, I made it so complex that he gave up. In January 1979, it was decided to empty the Olimpo and 'transfer' about one hundred people. I was transferred along with eight other prisoners to the División Cuatrerismo de Quilmes.

X96 was one of the few to survive that kind of "transfer."

One of the worst things was for a prisoner to discover that a wife, daughter or sister had also been arrested. Many of the chupados recounted how officials tormented them in interrogation sessions by bragging about having just pleasured themselves by raping their loved ones. The women had no choice: "Don't resist or we'll kill your husband." From time to time, officials would allow imprisoned couples to meet together. Husbands did not have to ask too many questions to realize that their boasts were actually true. Usually this was enough to extract some information in order to stop future rapes. It didn't matter [to the torturers] as every night fresh couples were brought into ESMA.

The parent factory

"Don't cut the cord, don't cut it!" she cried. But they were not tears of joy. And neither was it the pain of childbirth that made her despair. With her newborn baby held tight to her chest and still covered in blood, she screamed again with all the breath she had left: "Do not take away my baby!" But it ended as it had to end. Sara Solarz de Osatinsky spoke as a witness in one of the trials of the leaders of the Armed Forces. She described the hellish ESMA *escuela*, and how newborn babies were taken away from their mothers.

Sara's testimony was decisive in sentencing naval officer Jorge Acosta thirty years after the events. Known as "*El Tigre*," (the Tiger), he was sentenced together with Lieutenant Alfredo Astiz, the "blonde angel" who had infiltrated the parish of Santa Cruz.

Solarz de Osatinsky was the wife of a member of the Revolutionary Armed Forces who had been taken out by the junta. Both of her children, aged fifteen and eighteen, were also killed. She was picked up on the street and stripped and beaten before being thrown into a cell at ESMA.

Once someone entered the torture centers, they rarely escaped alive. It is estimated that around five thousand people entered ESMA alone. Only two hundred ever saw the light of day again.

"It was like a giant coffin," Solarz said during the trial describing the hellish female ward. "Everything was made of wood. The ceilings were so low that we were forced to remain lying down. In the midst of all this, there was this pregnant girl. I later learned that her name was Ana de Castro Rubel. There was not a birthing room yet when her baby boy was born. If there had been, the infant would have been taken away immediately. She kept asking me if I noticed a particular sign on the baby that she could later use to recognize him when she got out." Almost forty years have passed. Ana and her baby are both counted among the *desaparecidos*. She was killed—no one knows where—and her child was adopted by military order.

In revolting irony, the military nicknamed the ESMA birthing room the "little Sarda." The real "*Maternidad Sarda*," in fact, was a respected maternity clinic in a Buenos Aires public hospital. Pregnant women were transported to ESMA from detention centers around the country. Sara was not a midwife, but she helped fifteen women deliver babies they would never see and who would never know their real parents. "There were four beds. The first time, I went there with Maria Pichona. She wanted me to be close to her. I remember the awful noise of chains mixed together with the newborn baby's cries. When they took her baby away, she began to cry." She could do nothing else, "Why will they not let me stay with my little baby? Why?"

Due to her testimony as well as the tenacity of the *Abuelas* (the Grandmothers of Plaza de Mayo*), 150 of these children, mostly adopted by childless military families, came to know their true identity. There are at least 400 who still remain unknown.

Victoria Donda Pérez was able to reconstruct the story of her real family. She was born at ESMA where

---

* The Grandmothers of the Plaza de Mayo (Spanish: *Asociación Civil Abuelas de Plaza de Mayo*) is a human rights organization with the goal of finding missing children sequestered and adopted by military families during the Dirty War.

her parents were later tortured and killed. After Victoria's birth, her mother was put to death in the presence of an uncle who was a member of the secret police and later was put on trial. Before being taken to the gallows, the woman managed to pierce the earlobes of her newborn with a blue thread in an effort to be able to later recognize her. Victoria was adopted by a military family who renamed her Analía. The girl discovered her true identity only twenty-seven years later, thanks to an anonymous witness and to the Grandmothers of Plaza de Mayo.

"My story," Victoria explained while attending the trial against her uncle, "has been painful. The worst part was when I learned that I was the daughter of desaparecidos, and that my father's brother was present when they tortured my mother."

* * * * *

This was the Argentina of Jorge Mario Bergoglio who became provincial superior of the Jesuits of Argentina in 1973. It was a maze of twisted mirrors in which everyone was suspicious of everyone else and there seemed to be no way out. The country had fallen into the worst hands. It was run by double-crossers and opportunist careerists. The military coup d'état brought many inept (and worse) people to positions of power: thieves, ex-cons, hoodlums, gangsters and thugs. For many it was a way to earn amnesty or gain a certain amount of respect. Or it was a way to clear away the wreckage of their past and start over. All they had to do was stay on the bandwagon and never go against the flow. Many of them only had to change their clothes to continue to steal, beat, and rape: a uniform converted thugs into men of the state. You had to be careful around these people. But in order to save innocent lives, you had to know how to deal with them.

CHAPTER 3

BERGOGLIO HELPED THE VICTIMS, WHILE OTHER PRIESTS SUPPORTED THE REGIME

THE opinion of Professor Loris Zanatta is not gentle.

The history of the Argentine church is not a bed of roses. Less still is the history of Argentina. Rare are, therefore, those who come out clean. And even less so the handmaidens. Boasting its monopoly as a "Catholic nation," the church clung to the state for a long time and, within the state, to men in uniform. In the beginning, the church favored Peronist populism when it was initially taking off, only to later condemn it when it tried to squeeze the church within its totalitarian grip. Later, it became a handmaiden to the successive military governments after the fall of Peronism. Thus, for a long time the church and the military rose up together as bastions of order, willing to do anything to prevent the spread of "foreign" ideas within the *ser nacional* (national identity) which they safeguarded and against which they would not tolerate dissent. Needless to say, with such a background, a huge burden of culpability weighed heavily on the shoulders of the Argentine church, and her closets concealed skeletons. After the tremendous clamor of those violent years was over, the church was the first to return and ask forgiveness.

The professor of Latin American history at the University of Bologna says, however, that you have to ask yourself some questions. First, you have to have a realistic understanding of the social and political context. Zanatta says, "Did all this make the church complicit with Videla's regime? In part, yes. Certainly there were several bishops who were complicit, but more so were some military chaplains. And it was the burden of that long history that led the church to avoid public denunciations and condemnations, instead seeking to deal with regimes confidentially. But does this collective culpability pass, however, to every priest, including Bergoglio? Of course not."

These were times of stark contrast. Families were divided. So were politics. Zanatta continues, "The Argentine church was so divided during that period that it seemed split in half—what one hand was doing appeared hateful to the other. And then, there are those who knew Bergoglio at that time—from Nobel Prize winner, Pérez Esquivel, to former minister, Fernández Meijide. Even though they are critical of the church of that period, both exonerate the current pope. Not only that: they claim that the accusations that [Bergoglio] abandoned the two priests in the hands of the regime* are not at all true. From what I know, I can assure you that the Jesuits in Argentina, whose provincial superior was Bergoglio, were not timid in their dealings with Videla to secure the two priests' release."

It was a barbaric age. Even the international community sat on the sidelines while the dictatorship killed many innocent people. And as many as were guilty, just as many did not receive the justice they deserved. "Even the *Montoneros* guerrillas killed," recalls Zanatta. In fact, it was their propensity towards violence that led to the military coup in the first place. The revolutionaries believed that the people would then rise up [and support them in their fight against the government], but they were wrong. The vast majority of Argentines were exasperated by years of violence and ideology, and did not react to Videla's rise to power.

A perhaps little known fact is that many *Montoneros* were Catholics. "They, too, had their good chaplains to bless their arms. And many priests within the fervent revolutionary climate of that time supported the montonero cause. They were militant political activists dressed in a cassock," Zanatta notes. "And the dictatorship was fierce

---

* See the note on pg. 60 and the chapter "The Jalics-Yorio case" pp. 71–81; check page numbers

against them. Such was the point of division among the country as well as the church. And such was the morass that Argentina sank into. The revolutionaries of that time, who today are numerous in government corridors of power, do not forgive Bergoglio for the same reason they have never forgiven the church: because they [the church] caused Perón to fall in 1955. And at present on several occasions, they [the church including Bergoglio] have challenged Kirchner's government. In this, they forget that Peronism was popular but also totalitarian, and the criticisms of the Argentine government by the Archbishop of Buenos Aires in recent years are a healthy cost of democracy."

This is also behind the attacks against Bergoglio. "There is an obvious intent to discredit him by pigeonholing him in the past," Zanetta says. "These people who point their finger at the splinter in another's eye while ignoring the beam in their own eye no longer have before them an archbishop whom they hated so much, but now a pope. Baseless attacks against the pope may generate publicity for them, but they can also become a boomerang."

Tormenting chaplains

The life sentence of March 10, 2007 handed down against Christian Von Wernich, former chaplain of the Buenos Aires police department, reignited the controversy over the role played by the church during the military regime of 1976–83. In its comment on the sentence, the archdiocese of Buenos Aires (which Von Wernich belonged to), asked for "forgiveness and sincere repentance."

"We pray for him that God may help him and give him the necessary grace to understand and be aware of the damage he caused," the archdiocese said in a written statement. Cardinal Bergoglio wrote and signed the statement saying, "The pain that the participation of a priest in serious crimes causes us," requires "reconciliation." He insisted on one point: Argentina must be free of "impunity, hatred, as well as rancor."

Angela Boitano, the mother of two desaparecidos, recalls, "There have been cases of complicity [of some in the church] such as those of Von Wernich. Yet, at the same time many priests did not give in and instead fought against the horrors of the regime." The dark records of the Dirty War count at least twenty-four priests and religious either executed or missing, including, as we shall see, Bishop Enrique Angelelli and the group of Pallotine priests murdered between 1976 and 1977. This number does not include numerous priests who were arrested and interrogated.

The faults of the clergy were summarized in the dramatic *Nunca más* (Never Again), an extensive report (though by no means exhaustive), published in 1984 by the CONADEP commission. Known as the *Sábato Comisión* from the name of its chairman, writer Ernesto Sábato*, the commission was called for by newly elected

---

* Published in English by Farrar Straus with the title, *Nunca más* (*Never Again*). Rapporto della Commissione nazionale sulla scomparsa di persone in Argentina (1986).] The report is available online at: http://www.desaparecidos.org/nuncamas/web/english/library/nevagain/nevagain_000.htm

head of state, Raúl Alfonsín, in the early 1980s to investigate crimes committed during the dictatorship.

"From the enormous documentation examined by us (7,830 dossiers), it is clear that human rights were violated methodically by the state through repression carried out by the Argentine Armed Forces, not only sporadically, but systematically. . . . How can we not attribute this to a terror strategy organized at the highest level?"

An entire chapter is devoted to "The attitudes of some members of the Church":

> The bishops of the Argentinian Church repeatedly condemned the repression which this Commission investigated, said the text. Scarcely two months had passed since the coup on March 24, 1976 when the episcopal Conference described the [dictatorship's] methods as 'sinful' in a General Assembly. In May 1977, the episcopal Conference presented a strongly worded document along similar lines to members of the military junta.

The church's position was clear enough, however, "regrettably, some individual members of the clergy supported the very actions that had been condemned by the church as a whole through their presence, silence or even direct involvement."

Up until the launch of the report, CONADEP calculated that 8,960 people were considered missing. For the first time, twenty-four priests and religious "victims of repression" were added, as well as a yet undermined number of lay Catholics who had been secretly arrested never to return home. It would take years to arrive at a much more reliable estimate believed to be at least thirty thousand people "sucked up." The report describes in broad, stark terms how this happened:

> It began with the victim's arrest by agents who avoided identifying themselves. The abducted people were then taken to one of the 340 clandestine detention centers. These were headed by senior officers of the Armed Forces or security forces. The prisoners were kept in inhumane conditions and subjected to every kind of torture and humiliation.
>
> The evidence of widespread torture by sadistic torturers in these centers is terrible. There have been several cases of children and the elderly being tortured together with their family members so that they would provide their captors with information.

Testimonials incriminating members of the clergy are dramatic. With his head bowed down, Julio Alberto Emmed recounted his role in an incident involving a chaplain who was later sentenced to life imprisonment.

> In 1977, I was a policeman in the Buenos Aires province. At the end of 1977 or the beginning of 1978, I was summoned to the office of the Chief Inspector in the presence of Father Christian Von Wernich [...]. On another

occasion it was explained to us that we were to pick up three subversives who had been 'broken' in interrogation and had collaborated with the repressive forces in return for a promise that they would be transferred abroad.

The three victims had been promised freedom. But it was a trap.

We left in three cars. Father Christian Von Wernich was waiting for us at the Detective Squad at La Plata. He had spoken to and blessed the ex-subversives and had organized a farewell for them at the same unit. The family (who were to await them in Brazil) had sent them flowers. The three ex-subversives—two women and a man—were allowed to go free, without handcuffs, and as far as they were concerned we were simply guards who were to take them to the airport and put them on the plane. . . . Father Christian Von Wernich was in the car with me.

"The signal to start was a message we would receive on the radio asking our position," Emmed continued. "When we received the signal in car no. 3 I had to give the blow that would knock 'X' out. I hit him near the jaw but it did not knock him out." The other agent who was in the car "took out his issued gun." When the guy saw it he jumped on it and a fight ensued. "This forced me to grab him by the neck and I hit him several times on the head with the butt of my gun. This produced several wounds and he bled profusely; both the priest, the driver and the two of us who were beside him were bloodstained." The three cars went down a side street toward a wooded area where they waited for a medical officer.

"The three ex-subversives were still alive when they were taken out," testified Emmed. "They were thrown on the grass, the doctor gave them two injections each, directly in the heart, with a reddish poisonous liquid. Two died but the physician left all three for dead. They were loaded on to a van." Meanwhile, Julio Alberto Emmed and the chaplain went to change clothes and then reached the police station. "Father Von Wernich saw that what had happened had shocked me, and spoke to me telling me that what we had done was necessary; it was a patriotic act and God knew it was for the good of the country. Those were his very words."

Another witness, Luis Velasco, testified before the Sábato Comisión. He said that one day in one of the clandestine detention centers called La Casita, "after the first torture session, a priest came to me. I later learned that he was Christian Von Wernich." Velasco was a prisoner who was spared death. "Once I heard Von Wernich respond to an inmate who was pleading for his life: 'The life of men depends on God and your cooperation.'"

* * * * *

Adelina de Burgos Di Spalatro was a mother. She was desperate. She wanted to know the fate of her son, Óscar Carlos Lorenzo, who was arrested with other students. Monsignor Grasselli, secretary of the chaplain, "told us that some young people were in a program in homes created

for their rehabilitation. They were treated well there [...].
He told us that Videla was a charitable man who had come
up with this plan to avoid the 'loss' of intelligent people
[...]. He said that the work was performed by psycholo-
gists and sociologists, and that there were teams of doctors
present to look after their health. And for those who were
irreparable, 'some pious soul' would administer an injec-
tion to put them to sleep forever." In reality, such centers
for the "rehabilitation" of adversaries never existed.

The list of priests strongly suspected of connivance
with state criminals grew longer with each new deposition. "In the Caseros prison, around March of 1980,
I was subjected to torture sessions by the head of the
Inspectorate. It was accompanied by the head of the
guards and was in the presence of Father Cacabello," said
Eusebio Héctor Tejada.

Another man—a labor unionist named Plutarch
Antonio Schaller—said: "The chaplain Pelanda López visited me briefly on Sundays, chatting for a short while in
the cells." During one of these pathetic meetings, the prisoner begged him to intervene: "Father, they are torturing
me terribly during interrogations and I beg you to intercede to stop them from torturing me anymore." The priest
replied: "Well, my son, but what do you expect if you don't
cooperate with the authorities interrogating you?"

On another occasion the unionist said to the chaplain
that "they could not possibly continue to torture me as
they were doing," to which Pelanda López replied, "You
have no right to complain about the torture," with the
tone of someone sick and tired of his whining.

Were all the bishops accomplices?

The intervention of the triumvirate led by dictator Videla was welcomed by some people of good-will as a necessary shock to the country in order to restore stability and prevent Argentina from sliding into civil war. To others (and here there wasn't so much good-will), it was a bitter pill to swallow in order to stave off the menace of what was referred to as "tango-communism."

The leaders of the regime strutted around and flaunted their insignia claiming to have been called upon to put an end to unbearable domestic terrorism. In reality, they were hiding behind the façade of good intentions in an effort to control the entire country through their own systematic brutality.

The conference of bishops published a collective pastoral letter on May 15, 1976, in which they sought to denounce this dramatic historical event. The text had to carefully mediate among the various positions. Yet, in the end the regime laughed at them. The generals were convinced that the church hierarchy was mostly afraid and in some cases outright complicit, and thus posed no threat to them.

José Antonio Plaza, the archbishop of La Plata, is not remembered well. He was accused of having actively contributed to the forces of repression. His detractors blame him for having assisted in the arrest of dozens of people, including a young nephew of his, José María Plaza. In 1976, he was appointed major chaplain of the police of the Buenos Aires province, which at that time was controlled by a sadistic colonel named Ramón Camps. They were seen together in a number of detention and torture centers.

In 1983, two years after the fall of the regime and four years before his death, Plaza was interviewed by the newspaper, *La Voz*. The archbishop's opinion speaks for itself: "The condemnation of the military government is payback by subversives. This is Nuremberg in reverse. Those who defeated terrorism are now being judged by criminals."

In the early years of the junta, alarming reports began arriving in Rome. In accordance with what his brother priests at the Colegio Máximo confirmed, Bergoglio regularly kept his superiors at the Jesuit Generalate house in Rome informed. It is not too imaginative to assume that they, in turn, would have reported these events to the Secretary of State of the Holy See.

Pope Paul VI was alarmed at the information he received. On January 20, 1977, he received Bishop Plaza at the Vatican. The pontiff expressed his anxieties in the following question he posed to the bishop: "Is it true that despicable excesses are taking place in your country against people who are not terrorists but are opposed to the new military government?" It was obvious that fairly accurate reports had arrived in Rome and lacked only the countersignature of the Argentine bishop.

Plaza's reply was indignant: "No, your holiness. Nothing of the sort is taking place! These are false and unfounded rumors put into circulation by people who have fled [Argentina] and sought refuge in Europe."

PART TWO

THE STORIES

CHAPTER 4

GONZALO MOSCA

*The labor unionist pursued
by two dictatorships*

"MY days were numbered. I was desperate." The Uruguayan activist, Gonzalo Mosca, was in trouble because of his political beliefs. In 1977, Gonzalo was twenty-eight years old. At that time, the generals had been getting rid of dissidents with the same nonchalance as if swatting mosquitoes. The young Mosca belonged to the *Grupos de acción unificada*, a coalition of parties that helped found the "*Frente Amplio*" in 1971, a leftist organization that governed uninterruptedly in Montevideo from 1984 onwards, the year when Uruguay regained democracy.

Gonzalo decided to tell his story as soon as he saw the man who saved him on the television screen. Things in his home country had turned so bad for him that he had to take refuge in Argentina. Yet, he knew very little about the [Argentine] dictatorship. Mosca thought he would be able to disappear in the endless Buenos Aires suburbs and the vast *pampas*. Instead, he went from the frying pan into the fire.

He escaped Uruguay, where, in Montevideo, five military units had been deployed to watch over the eight clandestine prisons and the nine secret cemeteries, which since 1971 were used to bury [members of] the *"Juventud Comunista"* (Communist Youth), [which Mosca belonged to].

Once Mosca reached Buenos Aires, the disheveled young man took refuge in a friend's house. But his cover did not last long. "The Argentine army came looking for us. Fortunately, we had just left the apartment," says Mosca thirty-six years later.

The caretaker of the building had warned him: *"Te matarán."* ("They'll kill you.") In order not to end up dead, he had to choose a path which, for someone like him, was full of traps: ask help from the priests. With a public telephone, Gonzalo was able to call his brother—a Jesuit priest who was living in Argentina. Father Mosca could not give immediate help, but he knew where to turn.

A few days later, the young Jesuit reached the Argentine capital where his brother, *"compañero* Mosca," was watching the clock and hoping against destiny. He had only one doubt: would the soldiers of Buenos Aires kill him in Argentina or would he be sent back to suffer the scrupulous "care" of their Uruguayan cohorts?

When Fr. Mosca contacted the priest who had once been his professor of philosophy, the latter answered meticulously as if dictating a telegram. He did so whenever the situation was grave: "Bring me your brother, I will try to help." Father Bergoglio arrived by car at the agreed upon place. He was alone. I could still perceive what Gonzalo Mosca felt at that moment; his face lit up while speaking about it. That day, however, he could not bear the fear.

When recounted today, it seems like the impossible mission of a daring secret agent. Father Bergoglio knew Buenos Aires well, as he was born there and had lived there for forty years. He also knew the fixations, weaknesses, and habits of the military. "He told me not to look out the window as there were soldiers on practically every street corner." Mosca's fear increased and he felt like he was unable to breathe. The thirty miles seemed like three thousand—sudden turns, detours along back roads, Fr. Bergoglio's eyes constantly checking the rearview mirrors.

Churches were no longer places of refuge: the infiltrators had gotten to priests who were traitors, who were afraid, or who openly supported the regime. This was not difficult to do in that capital city with so many eyes and too many ears. Dark vans were everywhere; some were parked, others drove slowly. They were like packs of hunting dogs marking their territory. Their job was to instill fear by the mere fact of being in motion. No, you could not even trust going into a church. You did not know if he who entered to pray a *Pater*, an *Ave*, or a *Gloria* would leave an informant.

Buenos Aires is the perfect city to control militarily. Like many modern cities, the streets of the national capital are in a grid format giving no chances of surprise to the military: the city's blocks are squared; its streets fairly wide; there are no dark alleys; no maze of unpredictable trajectories. It is impossible to escape the firing squad. Those who live in Buenos Aires know that it is a labyrinth without secrets. The English know this as well, and also the Spaniards. The former were driven back into the sea with their garrisons in 1807; the latter were sent back on their caravels after the Revolution of May 1810, when the populace became a nation after choosing self-determination. And yet, in the years of the Dirty War, many pretended not to hear or to see. Even the church would be torn apart—with its credibility to regain and its community to rebuild.

It was not just the old Ford Falcons repainted green that struck terror in the hearts of the people. At least they were recognizable. The *patotas*—armed action groups of thugs and kidnappers in civilian clothes—instead were able to disguise themselves as motorists waiting in line for gas or as day laborers riding around in old beat-up trucks on the outskirts of the city.

Finally, something familiar made Gonzalo stop trembling. "My brother had studied with the Jesuits at San Miguel. I recognized it right away." Gonzalo did not stay for long at the Jesuit house. "At most four days," he told me. Father Bergoglio needed the time to organize his escape. "He introduced me as a student who was there for a brief retreat." All in all, it was not such a big lie.

Anyone who ended up there at the College in San Miguel with that unconventional Jesuit Bergoglio wondered what or even who would convince a young priest to risk his own skin and put his brother priests at risk. And he did so to save those with unorthodox beliefs, some of whom were essentially at odds [with the Church] to the point of even being anti-clerical. Gonzalo Mosca recalls, "While working on a solution to help me, Bergoglio came to check on me every evening. We would speak for a long time. He knew I was nervous and I couldn't sleep. He gave me some novels by [Jorge Luis] Borges and even a radio to pass the time and keep up on what was going on."

Helping dissidents escape was a risky operation; there was the real possibility of ending up directly in the hands of the torturers. Therefore, Father Jorge had built a support network in Brazil in order to improve the odds. In actuality, no one who belonged to the "Bergoglio system" knew they were a part of it. Each person performed a single task for the Argentine provincial in an organization made up of fixed sections: one person would offer a bed for a few nights; another would give someone a ride; someone else would put in a good word with the European consular officer; another person purchased the airline tickets. This was the best way to minimize risk and circulate as little information as possible—even among the Jesuits.

There was reason to be cautious. Throughout all of Latin America, a series of military coups took place one after another according to a certain order. In what was like the game of Risk, there was a coup in Brazil in 1964 and then the one in Argentina in 1976. In what came to be known as "Operation Condor," the military juntas of the entire subcontinent organized a wide-ranging crackdown to hunt down their foes.

According to independent studies, Uruguay, Brazil, Paraguay, Bolivia, in addition to Chile under Pinochet and Argentina under Videla all participated in the Condor Plan. The first working meeting of the secret services of countries participating in the Plan took place in Santiago, Chile, between November 25 and December 1, 1975, at the initiative of Manuel Contreras, the founder of General Pinochet's secret police. All this had the tacit consent of the United States who—after communism had been established in Cuba—sought to block the spread of socialism throughout the rest of the continent.

A former Brazilian general admitted that at the time of the dictatorships, agreements existed among various South American countries for the capture and return of dissidents to their country of origin. Former general, Agnaldo Del Nero, told the local press that "we did not kill" foes of other countries who took refuge in Brazil, "rather, the goal was to catch them and return them" to their nations of origin. In the 70s and 80s, he led the State Information Center (CIE) of São Paulo. Del Nero stated that when the Brazilian military received information about a foreign suspect who was about to enter their country, protocol called for their arrest and return. "And this is what happened to those two Italians," he noted in reference to two Italo-Argentines—Horacio Campiglia and Domingo Lorenzo Vinas—who were Montonero militants. Campiglia was captured in March of 1980 at the Galeão airport of Rio de Janeiro after departing from Venezuela. Vinas was arrested in June, 1980 in Uruguaiana in the state of Rio Grande do Sul.

We can thus fairly easily assume what Jorge Mario Bergoglio's fears would have been given that Argentina bordered countries that were also under military control. Yet Brazil, due to its size and large presence of Jesuits, lent itself more than the other countries in providing shelter to fugitives. In any case, however, international flights were out of the question.

Father Jorge was up to date and knew what was going on. While Gonzalo Mosca was holed up in a room at the College of San Miguel, the head of the Argentine Jesuits was developing a plan consisting of three stages that would lead the young militant to freedom. "You will take a plane from Buenos Aires to Puerto Iguazú, bordering Brazil and Paraguay. From there you will enter Brazilian territory." With a domestic airline ticket, Mosca would reach the northern border [of Argentina]. The crossing would have to take place by boat secretly. Once in Brazil, the Uruguayan would be taken care of by other Jesuits. Then after a short stay, they would put him on a flight to Europe. It was an amazing plan.

In order for it to work, Gonzalo would have to overcome a series of obstacles that made him tremble just to think about: Do not give the airport agents in Buenos Aires cause for suspicion; avoid the Argentine and Brazilian border guards; go back as far as Rio de Janeiro if you have to in order to avoid checkpoints; finally, reserve your airline flight or passage by ship to Europe only after first receiving clearance by the appropriate consular authorities of the chosen country for exile.

The young Uruguayan trusted him. "Father Jorge not

only drove me to the airport, but he accompanied me to the door of the plane." Bergoglio left the airport only after the aircraft had taken off.

The plan went precisely according to the provincial's plan: Gonzalo crossed at the Rio Paraná, not far from the majestic waterfalls of Iguazú where he could reach Brazil or Paraguay by going upstream. From there, he took part in another period of "spiritual formation" at a Jesuit community in Rio de Janeiro. In the end, he finally arrived at his destination overseas.

Today Gonzalo Mosca is a well-known labor unionist. He still works on behalf of Uruguayan workers as he did then. He is still not a typical churchgoer type of person. At least not until he saw an extraordinary priest become pope.

There were at least two hundred desaparecidos in his country, proportionally smaller than the elimination of opponents in neighboring Argentina. But even in Uruguay thousands of people were persecuted, and just as many fled abroad. The procedures for creating desaparecidos in Montevideo were subsequently perfected by the Videla junta.

Compañero Mosca asks himself, "I've always wondered if Bergoglio was fully aware of the risks he took. If we had been caught, he would have been accused of protecting a subversive and thus would have jeopardized the entire Jesuit institution." At that time the authorities did not suspect anything. "I don't know of other people who would have done the same thing. I don't know if anyone else would have saved me without knowing me at all."

To anyone who asks for an explanation, Mosca responds, "I received a Catholic education from the Jesuits. My brother is a Jesuit. These are their values. Inasmuch as I know them, this is how they are."

CHAPTER 5

ALICIA OLIVEIRA

Underground with Father Jorge

"NO one needs to tell me who Jorge Bergoglio is. He brought many persecuted people to safety outside the country and in the process put his own life in jeopardy. What else do they want?" Alicia Oliveira was the first woman to become a criminal court judge in Argentina in 1973. But the military wanted her out, and in 1976 she became the first female judge kicked out by the government. She was removed from office, fired by the Minister of Justice, and hunted by the police. These are all histories which she would have done without, but all things considered, now make her proud.

"All of a sudden, I found myself unemployed. When Jorge learned I had been fired, he sent me a beautiful bouquet of roses," Oliveira recalled in a long interview with *Clarín*, the largest Argentine newspaper.

A few minutes after the election of the Roman pontiff, Alicia's phone started ringing off the hook. Countless journalists asked her opinion of the new pope. She replied, "My opinion is that of a friend. For me, Jorge is a friend—not a cardinal, nor the pope. I have the highest regard for him. He is a great man, and is concerned for all who suffer." When I contacted her a few months later to have her reconstruct her tribulations during this period, she politely asked to be able to remain silent. "It has already been discussed enough." In several interviews and court depositions she had spoken of Bergoglio.

She met him during the era of the persecutions. Videla himself personally ordered that she be removed along with other activists of CELS (Center for Legal and Social Studies) which had become a thorn in the side of the military. They prepared a plot for her in the cemetery. But thanks to Father Jorge, the regime ended up duped.

The signal was a military blitz. When they raided the offices, they hauled off everyone who was there. Those not present were hunted down in their homes. "I managed to get away," Alicia recounts. "I had just left CELS for the train station moments before the soldiers swooped in. When I heard what happened, I had to find a hideout until the situation calmed down."

Hiding out was not something Alicia Oliveira was prepared for. It caused her numerous hardships, especially since she was the mother of three young children. Her son had a recurring nightmare and would wake up at night screaming that the soldiers had taken away his mommy. While on the run, Alicia was forced to stay away from her children. Those were terrible days—staying away from the regime and at the same time reassuring her children that their mommy would not be taken prisoner or end up desaparecida. The thought that they could be so traumatized kept her up at night, as well.

Oliveira had known Bergoglio for about four years. They had become friends, even though she was not a regular churchgoer. As always in such cases, Father Jorge was kind but straightforward. "Your life is in danger," he told her. He offered her a solution: "Come and stay with us at the college. You will be able to see your children there and remain safe. Then we will try to figure out how to resolve your situation." Yet Alicia responded, "I'd rather stay locked up in my hideout rather than live with the priests." There was no way to convince her to change her mind.

At that point Father Bergoglio could have said goodbye, wished her well, remembered her in his prayers, and moved on. He had done what he could to help her and certainly would not have felt any guilt had she refused him out of anticlerical contempt. There would be others—many others—who needed to be saved, and he could not waste his time pleading for someone to grab the life preserver he had thrown. Instead, Father Jorge resolved to do everything he could. He found a way to alleviate at least some of her pain. Through a secret passageway inside the college—one that only a few knew of—he devised a way for Alicia to meet with her children.

Such meetings were not without risks, however. Father Jorge had to pick her up by car at the agreed upon place. He was very good at driving. Between one curve and another, perhaps he prayed. Sometimes he changed direction as if he did not know where he was going. The dark sedan he drove did not attract attention. Meanwhile, he meticulously monitored his speed. He was not the type of driver to speed. If the agents had stopped him, it not only would have looked bad, but who knows what questions they would have asked. Everyone who drove fast was considered suspect—imagine a Jesuit. Father Jorge had to consider all these things. So, he made sure he was not followed. And then, what would they have thought at the discovery of a woman in the trunk or curled up in the back seat? The regime would certainly have enjoyed watching his downfall due to a woman. Imagine the front page headlines and the evening news controlled by the junta: "Leader of the Argentine Jesuits surprised with championess of human rights."

But he did not consider these things. He was interested only in not creating risks for Alicia and not scaring her children. Who knows how many times he thanked Providence when they arrived safe at the *Colegio Máximo.*

"That is how he took me from my hideout to the college." In the course of those two months, he undertook that perilous trip at least ten times—sometimes twice a week. It was frequent enough so that Alicia Oliveira had no doubts as to whose side the Creator was on.

Her story is verified by an authoritative and independent eyewitness—the current Security Minister of Argentina, Nilda Garré. She played a role in the formative years of the career of the current President of Argentina, Presidenta Cristina Fernández de Kirchner (notoriously not so friendly with Bergoglio). Nilda is an old friend of

Alicia Oliveira. In fact, it was Garré, above all, who was her accomplice during her two months of hiding and hid Oliveira when she was sought by the police.

"Jorge had terrible opinion of the dictatorship—the same that I had," assures Alicia Oliveira. The attacks leveled at him before and after his election to the throne of Peter were "a real disgrace, political accusations. But he never wanted to intensify the situation."

When the situation became less dangerous for her, she was able to ride with Bergoglio without having to stay out of sight. The military believed they had prevailed— Alicia was just another educated unemployed woman. And neither was the provincial superior of the Jesuits the public enemy number one in their eyes.

Once one of the most vociferous accusers of Bergoglio, journalist and former *Montonero*, Horacio Verbitsky*, said that the Jesuit "is an actor." He was right, but not in the way he meant. In fact, Father Bergoglio was able to trick the military into believing that he was

---

* Author of *El Silencio* (The Silence), Fandango Books, 2006. He was suspicious of Bergoglio based on the testimony of two priests abducted and then released, Fathers Yorio and Jalics (see pp. 67–75 in this book. After the election of Pope Francis, he renewed his allegations in the newspaper, *Página 12*. But in the following days, Father Jalics (Yorio died in 2000) told the media that he now considered it a mistake to continue to maintain that his abduction and that of Yorio in 1976 had taken place due to the denunciation of the then Jesuit provincial superior (Bergoglio). Verbitsky then admitted that the latter declaration of Jalics absolved Bergoglio of all responsibility. See H. Verbitsky, *Pasado pisado* in: www.pagina12.com.ar/diario/elpais/1-216255-2013-03-21.html

sitting around idly in the college waiting for the winds of calm to blow, all the while he was building a clandestine network giving cover to and rescuing dozens of people.

"We saw each other twice a week," recalled Alicia Oliveira. "He accompanied priests; he trusted me and let me know what was going on. When someone had to leave the country because he could not stay in Argentina one minute longer, there was a farewell lunch. And Bergoglio was always there."

There's more. Years later, details were discovered that could be the climax of a Hollywood thriller. President Videla plotted his sinister plans from the halls of the Casa Rosada, less than two hundred meters from the cathedral, both on the attractive Plaza de Mayo [square]. Along the street leading to the district of Monserrat a few steps away is the [Jesuit] church of St. Ignatius of Loyola with its adjoining residence and catholic school. This is where Bergoglio met with Alicia Oliveira along with other persecuted people. There, farewell lunches took place for those waiting to go below deck undercover in a fruit or merchandise boat in the hour-long journey between Buenos Aires and Uruguay. The military would never have imagined that Bergoglio would have attempted all this right under their noses. Father Provincial and the horde of dissidents he protected would have been too bold to do these things in front of the Casa Rosada. No one would have had the guts to do this. No one would have imagined that the church of St. Ignatius had become the nerve center for Bergoglio's "list."

CHAPTER 6

ALFREDO SOMOZA

The scholar saved without his knowledge

H E was just a boy when he found himself in the crosshairs of the police. And he remained there for a long time—all the way through the University. He loved history and literature. He mimeographed a literary magazine called *Viramundo* which attracted other book-loving adolescents. This was too much for the military junta, obsessed with building a new order based on anni-hilating the past and brainwashing the masses.

"In the beginning, no one believed these things were actually happening. No one knew about the clandestine prisons or the desaparecidos. We thought they were being taken away somewhere, imprisoned maybe, or even 'reed-ucated.'" Alfredo Somoza is now a respected journalist and an expert on international politics. He lives in Italy in Milan, where, among other things, he is president of the *Istituto cooperazione economica internazionale* (ICEI) (International Institute of Economic Cooperation).

When he speaks about that period, he shows no trace of melancholy. His tone and words are detached in the manner of an objective analyst. Like a surgeon inserting his scalpel, he explained, "Under any regime, the Church chooses a low profile. This allows it to operate as best as possible and remain close to its values." In the case of Argentina, however, "the ecclesial institution was strongly compromised by the dictatorship. But not the Jesuits. The story of the university where I was allowed to study—me, who was considered a dissident—is striking. They saved many lives. And I was an eyewitness."

With the eye of a journalist and the mind of a scholar, Somoza is an exceptional person. He does not claim himself to be a persecuted Christian. Nor does he play the part of the indomitable foe forced into exile. And yet, his story is exemplary.

He came from a good family. Since high school he had a passion for literature, anthropology, and archaeology. He was the perfect subversive . . . at least in the mind of the military. After various intimidations, he was dragged into a police station in 1978 where they held him for a week. It was just enough time to decide into which clandestine detention center to transfer him.

Somoza lived in a spacious house in Villa Devoto—a well-off neighborhood on the edge of the endless province of Buenos Aires. Once known for its green spaces, today it is swallowed up in urban sprawl. He attended the Jesuit *Universidad del Salvador* in San Miguel (University of the Salvador) during the years of the dictatorship when the future pope was provincial head of the Jesuit Society of Jesus. "That was the only university in Buenos Aires where dissidents could study." The state university had been "sterilized": Marx and any reference to the political left had been banned. The National Reorganization Process was achieved by breaking down the country's cultural centers, which would henceforth be controlled by men in green.

Why someone with a passion for antiquity would be considered a subversive is not hard to understand. "In my case, it was not healthy to go to the state university. I had had some problems, let's call them, while I was in high school. I was a student delegate then—a role of little importance. And yet, it was enough to end up on the black list of subversives. Unfortunately, I was not the only one in that situation. For people like me, there were only two choices: leave school or enroll at the Jesuit university."

In actuality, the administration of the Universidad del Salvador had been given over to the laity, "but it still remained under the direct influence of the Jesuits, and this preserved it from the influence of the regime. It was a kind of 'cultural free zone.'" Even if he did not have an official title, Father Bergoglio was a kind of "Rector *in pectore*" [secretly appointed].

Alfredo Somoza pointed out: "I'm not a believer nor have I ever been baptized. But, I can tell you that at the Universidad del Salvador, there was an atmosphere of freedom as in no other place in Buenos Aires. Its academic autonomy remained intact. While I was there, it seemed like the regime did not exist. The state university, however, had to close several departments such as sociology and anthropology which were considered a breeding ground for political foes."

When Videla and his cohorts took over the country, Alfredo was eighteen years old. At twenty, "he was abducted and detained in a police station." It was 1978. "I stayed there for a week in a type of limbo not knowing what would become of me." While the soldiers were discussing whether to send him to ESMA, Olympus, or some other slaughterhouse, someone—whose name is better to remain anonymous—"managed to get me out just in time before I 'disappeared.'"

"Then when the time for university came," Somoza recalls, "my situation was more open-ended. At the Universidad del Salvador, thanks to Bergoglio, we were in a kind of protective bubble. The junta had eliminated and banned any kind of organized representation by unions or students. We had to adapt even in our department." Bergoglio took the dictates of the regime very seriously. At least, he wanted to give this impression.

"In reality, the Jesuits were operating behind the scenes, as in the case of the two arrested priests [Fathers Yorio and Jalics, author's note] who were tortured and freed after six months and whose story was told by journalist Horacio Verbitsky. This has been discussed throughout the world. Verbitsky wondered if Bergoglio should be held accountable for their arrest. I think, on the contrary, that it was thanks to his efforts and those of all the Jesuits that the two men came out alive. And this was a time in which it was much more common to disappear forever," observes Somoza.

Today Alfredo is fifty-five years old, yet the poison of the regime did not cause him premature aging. In ways that are gentle, but firm, Somoza is not one to take things lightly. His radio program and his numerous essays are cordial but merciless against unrestrained capitalism and social injustice. He has remained the same as he was during his stint at the university.

"I studied archaeology with the Jesuits [at the Universidad del Salvador], because for us that was and is the university of the Jesuits. There, no one asked you for your baptismal certificate or criminal record. Right away, the junta abolished any form of representation. The Universidad del Salvador was also obliged to comply with the new laws. But you know how the Jesuits are. Once, Bergoglio made it clear in carefully chosen words that they would like for us students to 'confidentially' choose someone to represent us [in student unions or organized representation]. In an equally informal manner, the [Jesuits] would occasionally come talk with us." This was a way to circumvent the silly dictates of the military [ban on association] without risking people involved.

"This is how I met Father Bergoglio. He always counseled us not to risk it, that it wasn't worth it—in the sense that violence would not have resolved anything. He tried to dissuade us from getting into trouble. It was like hanging out with a friend at a coffee bar. He talked about football [soccer], about this and that. Then with that light-heartedness of his, but with a serious look, he said something far from superficial. It was his catchphrase with the students: 'No te la creas,' he repeated."

This phrase of his became like a mantra among the students. It was a kind of motto or slogan they would say to one another when they would meet on the streets or in rare moments of recreation. "'No te la creas' means 'don't believe it,' but it also means, 'do not be presumptuous or assuming.' Bergoglio was warning us with those words." It was as if he were saying: "Boys, do not trust everything people say around you; do not believe statements that you cannot verify and that are not convincing; but neither should you presume to know everything."

It was strange that a priest spoke that way during that infamous period in Argentina. "But he was Bergoglio, and we already knew that behind his jovial aspect, his informal ways, and sometimes his apparent naivety, was a man you did not mess with."

Information throughout the country was entirely controlled by the junta. Newspapers and television were nothing more than weapons of mass propaganda. "But the university was a life raft for us; it saved culture as well as—in my case—lives."

The repressive machine was traveling at full throttle. Somoza's mimeograph, too, was printing with steadfast regularity. It published works on poetry, literature, and a little bit of history. But not politics. Yet, the innocent paper, which was published independently, was soon considered subversive. "After controlling the flow of information, the dictatorship banned any new publication. There was nothing left for us to do other than mimeograph illegally," says Somoza. However, this was an outrage the military would not tolerate.

The moment arrived through a correspondence in 1981. Tensions within the military leadership had culminated with the passing of power from General Videla to Viola. The regime was in trouble, and their repression had become even more ruthless. A strange note arrived at Somoza's house. "My presence was requested in a government office to investigate some unidentified issue that concerned me." It was not difficult to understand. "The Secret Services had ascertained who was behind the clandestine newspaper. The letter was signed by the President of the Republic himself, General Viola, who personally invited me to participate in this meeting."

"I could not stay in Argentina one moment longer," says Alfredo. "I told my friends, and then I hopped on a boat from Buenos Aires to Uruguay, the ones that take less than an hour." Alfredo informed a few trusted people that he would go up to São Paulo, Brazil. "When I was a boy I had gotten my boating license. It was clear that I had closed the door on Argentina and my university studies, perhaps forever. So I decided to look for a job in the port city of Santos."

Alfredo decided to go it alone without help. "When I arrived in São Paulo, something happened that I still cannot explain today. It seemed like a lot of people were looking for me [to help]. I was contacted by people in touch with the Brazilian Jesuits and others from the curia of the São Paulo diocese. I found myself taking part in this network of refugees (not only from Argentina), which was managed by the Archdiocese of São Paulo and organized by Cardinal Arns. I went to a 'safe house' that took in refugees like me. And all this took place despite the fact that there was also a dictatorship in Brazil. But to me—accustomed to the repression in Argentina— Brazil appeared rather generous. The diocese of São Paulo, which worked with the UN agency for refugees (UNHCR), offered us a little financial support. They gave so much that the United Nations continuously sent people asking for help directly to the institutions of the church."

During that period, Somoza had not yet obtained an Italian passport. UN officials advised him against asking for political asylum in Brazil. The reality was that some- one had already thought about it. "I learned from the diocese of São Paulo that a secret escape had been pre- pared for me with the complicity of the representatives, a well-known Italian shipping company. For some time they had been hiding people in their cargo vessels and bringing them to safety in Europe."

The journey lasted a month. "They even allowed me to stay in the cabin normally reserved for the owner. I was to land in Genoa and then take the train to Milan where I would start my life over. Only later did I find out that I was not the only one who was assisted in this way. Many others had been through the same process."

But a question remained: who was behind this elab- orate system of rescues, economic assistance, and the organization of illegal extraditions? "After some insight, we came to the conclusion that all this unexpected assis- tance involved people who had studied with the Jesuits or who had been in contact with them. Actually, we only discovered this much later. Others arrived in Italy with passports issued by former Italian consul Enrico Calamai—now decorated with the highest honor in Argentina—who helped those persecuted escape the country. And he did so in defiance of the 'official' position of the embassy. Here, too, Jesuits were involved in 'presenting' some people to the consul."

"Who was head of the Jesuits in Argentina? Is it logical to imagine that all this happened without his direct involvement?" Somoza asked. "Bergoglio intervened in numerous cases. I remember a girl who suddenly disappeared. Father Jorge personally got involved in her case, but then he managed to find out that she had been shot dead in the course of a raid. It was not good news. Yet just discovering what happened to one of the desaparecidos was next to impossible. In another case, a student received assistance to get to Córdoba where the Jesuits had set up an organization to help those persecuted in Argentina as well as Paraguay escape abroad—usually to Brazil."

Having personally lived in that cruel period of history, Somoza argues that to try to "reduce—even symbolically—the value of the election [to the papacy] of Cardinal Jorge Mario Bergoglio, Archbishop of Buenos Aires, to the controversy over his alleged faults during the military dictatorship reveals a very limited vision of the challenges this pontificate will face." Under the dictatorship, the church in Argentina "was divided between a small minority of people who resisted and for the most part were killed by the military, a significant part of the hierarchy that was guilty of direct complicity, and an 'indefinite' part, made up of priests and religious who, although not publically condemning the regime, neither approved it either and often managed to save the lives of many people." Bergoglio and the Jesuit Company of Jesus "are certainly counted among these."

CHAPTER 7

THE JALICS-YORIO CASE

"We were not denounced by Bergoglio"

A "CLASSIFIED" document has reemerged within the archives of the Secret Service, and for years has been considered valid: A top secret folder with the cold title, "Directorate of Religion, binder 9, file B2B, Archdiocese of Buenos Aires, document 9." In the document, the Argentine political police stated: "Despite the good will of Father Bergoglio, the Argentine Company [*author's note: this is a reference to the Jesuits*] has not cleaned house. Shrewd for some time, the Jesuits have remained on the sidelines, but now with strong support from the outside by certain Third World bishops, they have begun a new phase." To what extent the evaluations of the spies of a dictatorial regime are objective, fair and reliable remains to be seen.

At that time, words were fired like bullets. In the years of General Videla's military junta, the mud-slinging machine worked handily. This confidential document insinuates that Father Bergoglio collaborated with the regime. But why would the Secret Service have written, "Despite the good will of Father Bergoglio" in a file that could fall into hostile hands? It doesn't add up. The secret file does not assign a nickname or protected identity to the "Bergoglio Source," even though code names were used for other informants and double agents. If the Jesuit provincial had been a useful informant, why would a regime so careful at protecting itself have run the risk of exposing him?

The accusation of a scheming Bergoglio does not hold up for another reason: how can they count among their collaborators someone who "did not clean house"? In the file, the Jesuits are accused of not having corrected their direction toward the "Third World Movement," instead of toward the military junta. Who would have indicated this direction other than Bergoglio himself who was their leader in Argentina? The reference to "good will" thus appears to be slanderous mudslinging written during the era of the regime in order to undermine Bergoglio's credibility. Or it could have been written to allow for an eventual vendetta at some point in the future. Indeed, both happened to Bergoglio.

In 2010, when asked by a federal tribunal as a "person informed of the facts," the future pope confirmed to the authorities what he had hitherto only confided to his closest friends*. He revealed that he had saved many dissidents. But publically, he had never spoken of it on any occasion.

---

* Refer to the ESMA trial transcripts in the Appendix.

"I hid some of them in the Jesuit Colegio Máximo of San Miguel in the region of Gran Buenos Aires where I lived," said the former Cardinal. "I do not remember exactly how many. After the death of Bishop Enrique Angelelli [the bishop of La Rioja murdered for his efforts defending the poor], I took three seminarians from his diocese who were studying theology into the college. They were not hidden, but cared for and protected, yes."

The story of the three seminarians told in this book on pages 91–106 emerged a few years earlier when the bishop of Bariloche, Monsignor Fernando Maletti, became aware of it. But Bergoglio did not use the opportunity to silence or even cast doubts on the allegations that were then swirling against him. He had neither the desire nor the time to care about his image.

Various accusations against Bergoglio propagated by the regime have been taken at face value by foes as well as victims of the dictatorship. They continue to this day as "weeds among the wheat." As soon as he was elected Pope Francis, various articles from the *New York Times* to the Argentine daily *Página 12* were run thus reviving suspicion on his "complicity" with the regime. According to statements gathered by journalist Horacio Verbitsky (in the end retracted) (see footnote on p. 55), in the summary of the BBC, Bergoglio "removed his protection of two priests who worked in the slums" of Buenos Aires which distanced them from the Jesuits and exposed them to military reprisals.

The cardinal "in 2010 was called to testify in the case: he stated that he had asked the leaders of the regime to release" the two priests. As the BBC highlighted, they were then freed. According to the British network, investigators also questioned the future pope regarding "the case of Elena de La Cuadra, daughter of one of the cofounders of the *Abuelas de Plaza de Mayo* who disappeared while she was pregnant." Finally, according to the BBC, Bergoglio was also cited in a criminal case opened in France regarding the abduction and murder of the priest, Gabriel Longueville, in 1976. In the end, the courts reached the long overdue conclusion that his actions did not warrant culpability.

The military dictatorship's plot to make Father Bergoglio appear "affiliated" with the regime was an attempt to tarnish his reputation. They wanted to discredit him as "unreliable" in the eyes of dissidents and his fellow Jesuits. Such a technique was not at all new. In Poland, as in communist Hungary and Romania, the same thing happened to priests and intellectuals who did not give in [to the respective regimes]. Seeds of doubt planted in public opinion can sometimes be more effective than intimidation and ruthless interrogations.

"Was Pope Francis close to the military dictatorship in Argentina? Not at all." When I met Adolfo María Pérez Esquivel, a human rights activist and winner of the Nobel Peace Prize in 1980 for his denunciations of military abuses, he was staunch in his defense of Bergoglio. He did not hesitate to state that in the church, "There were clergymen who were accomplices of the dictatorship," but he assures that "Bergoglio was not one of them." The former archbishop of Buenos Aires, "is accused of not having done what was necessary to secure the release of the two priests [*author's note: in reality they eventually freed, with enormous help from Bergoglio*] while he was superior of the Jesuit order. But I know personally many bishops who asked the military junta to liberate prisoners and priests, yet their request was not granted."

Even Graciela Fernández Meijide, a former member of the National Commission on the desaparecidos created after Argentina's return to democracy, is categorical: "There is no evidence that Bergoglio collaborated with the dictatorship. I know this personally. I suffered the loss of a child. My friend, Pérez Esquivel, was almost killed by the military. But you cannot say that all priests were accomplices of the dictatorship. That is absurd."

Among former dissidents, however, there are discordant voices. Estela Carlotto is the leader of the Grandmothers of Plaza de Mayo. Immediately after white smoke arose from the Sistine Chapel, she said she did not have a clear opinion on the actions "of Pope Francis at the time of the dictatorship. The important thing for me, however, is knowing that the pope desires to promote peace, brotherhood, and love of neighbor." A few weeks later, Estela Carlotto would be received by Pope Francis in a private audience.

In the timeframe between the pope's election and their meeting, I published the first counter argument against the mudslinging at the former provincial of the Jesuits in the newspaper, *Avvenire*. In a five-part series, the other side began to emerge slowly until the conclusion that caused Verbitsky to withdraw his previous allegations.

On April 24, Bergoglio met Carlotto face-to-face. "There are still criticisms; history is not erased in one embrace. But the criticism was constructive and not absolute. Truth does not offend," said the leader of the Grandmothers of the Plaza de Mayo. "On our side, there is no hatred or resentment. But the reality of state terrorism is a documented fact that one cannot dispute, and the church knew about it." However, Carlotto expressed "great satisfaction, because my meeting with the pope gave us hope that we can open a pathway to find the children and grandchildren of those who disappeared. . . . We do not blame Bergoglio. What we seek and ask for is that these 'grandchildren' may come to know their fathers and mothers. The church knows. It can help with its records." The response of the pope was more than a promise: "Count on me."

Also fueling the dark legend of Bergoglio as "traitor priest" are some carefully prepared photographs. In the original caption of one shot in which Videla receives communion from a priest shown from behind, there is no reference to Bergoglio. Though it was 1990 and the Jesuit was fifty-four years old, the image shows a fairly old celebrant handing the host to the general. "Former Argentine President Jorge Rafael Videla receives communion in a church of the Roman Catholic rite in Buenos Aires in this picture dated December 20, 1990," reads the caption in the original snapshot kept by the photographic agency Corbis. Yet, conveniently cropped in such a way as to make it practically impossible to identify the officiant, this case was passed along as the lynchpin of proof of

Bergoglio's alleged closeness to the regime even after the dictatorship's fall in 1983. Another falsehood.

The truth has been slow to emerge just as in the case of the two Jesuits supposedly "sacrificed" by their provincial superior. Slowly, pain has given way to peace in what Father Franz Jalics now considers a "settled affair," and he finally feels "reconciled to those events." Father Jalics was a Hungarian Jesuit missionary in Argentina during the military dictatorship. He wished to write the words "the end" in his own hand to the fictitious story of Bergoglio as a man so scornful that he would hand over his two brother priests to the military police.

Father Jalics was known by everyone in Buenos Aires as Francisco. He was one of the two missionaries arrested and tortured for nearly six months in 1976 on charges of supporting communist guerrillas. According to local sources, Pope Francis did not protect Fathers Jalics and Yorio.

The elderly Hungarian priest wrote in a brief memoir in German: "In 1957, I relocated to Buenos Aires. In 1974, I felt moved by an inner desire to live the Gospel and make people aware of the conditions of appalling poverty. With the permission of Archbishop Aramburu and then Father [provincial] Jorge Bergoglio, I lived with a brother priest in a shantytown. From there, however, we continued our teaching in the university."

Trouble for the two frontier priests began right away. "The military junta had killed about three thousand people—leftist guerrillas as well as innocent civilians. The two of us had no contacts either with the junta or the guerrillas in the slums." However, "due to lack of information and because of false information purposely provided, our position was misunderstood—even within the church." This argument would be used by Bergoglio's accusers to count him as an accomplice of the regime.

"At that time," recalls Father Jalics, "we lost touch with one of our lay associates who had joined the guerrillas." She had probably gone underground, but was arrested nine months later. Following "her interrogation by junta soldiers, they learned that we had worked together. This is why we were arrested—on the assumption that we had ties with the guerrillas."

"The officer who questioned me asked to see some identification," recalls the eighty-six-year-old Father Jalics. "When he saw that I was born in Budapest, he thought I was a Russian spy." But our release seemed imminent: "After five days, the officer who conducted the interrogation left telling us: 'Fathers, you have no fault. I will work to get you back to your slums.' Despite that commitment, we remained imprisoned—inexplicably to us—for another five months, blindfolded and with our hands tied."

Jalics and Yorio were released after months of torture at ESMA. In a response during his questioning at the ESMA trial in 2010*, Bergoglio said that he switched places with a military chaplain and personally met with General Videla asking for the immediate release of his two brother priests. "I am reconciled to those events, and for me the issue is closed," reiterated Father Jalics. The other priest who was with him, Father Orlando Yorio,

---

*   see Appendix

died of natural causes in 2000. "After our liberation," says Father Franz, "I left Argentina. Only years later did I have the chance to talk with Father Bergoglio about those events, who in the meantime had been appointed archbishop of Buenos Aires. After that meeting, we celebrated Mass together in public and embraced one another solemnly." It was a gesture performed intentionally before the people to stop the slander.

On March 15, 2013, Father Jalics stated that he had been "reconciled" with his provincial superior and to the events of the 1970s. The elderly priest returned to the subject two days after his statement had been made public by Jesuit leaders, as some in the media continued to equivocate. Jalics recalled, among other things, that both among the Argentine Jesuits as well as "in church circles, false information was spread that we had been sent to the slums so that we would seem to be taking part in the guerrilla war." These rumors were circulated quite well, but they confirm that it is "false to believe that our arrest took place due to the instigations of Father Bergoglio. Orlando Yorio and I were not denounced by Bergoglio." These nine words conclude years of controversy.

It was the torturers who led the two prisoners to believe they had been "sold out" by their provincial, Father Jorge. This was nothing more than typical slander and defamation practiced by dictatorial regimes everywhere. "I did believe that we were the victims of a false accusation," reiterated Jalics, "but by the end of the nineties, thanks to several meetings, it was clear that such an assumption was unfounded."

CHAPTER 8

CHALLENGING THE ADMIRAL

T HE charges levied against the former provincial "were carefully examined by us," explained Germán Castelli, one of the three judges in the trial against the ESMA militants. "We examined all the data and came to the conclusion that the actions of Bergoglio had no judicial significance."

"To say that Jorge Bergoglio handed over those priests is absolutely false," repeated the magistrate.

The cardinal of Buenos Aires did not shy away from a barrage of questions before the Argentine investigators, replicated on April 23, 2011 by the federal court no. 6 with thirty-three questions to which the future pontiff responded in writing.

"I did what I could—what was in my ability according to my age then and the few relationships I had, in order to intercede to free those being held," said Bergoglio. In fact, as the Jesuit who would become pope stated, "I saw General Jorge Videla and Admiral Emilio Massera on two occasions though it was difficult then to get a hearing with them." Both tried to send him down the wrong path.

The young provincial of the Argentine Jesuits was studying the situation. As he said, he wanted to save those who were imprisoned. But he also wanted to keep traitors at bay; he did not know who they were or how they were getting information out. Therefore, he suggested that his brother priests move with extreme caution, and he devised a series of tricks to keep mail and telephone communications free from military control. During this period, Father Jorge regularly informed the Jesuit headquarters in Rome. They sent him an urgent request: "Protect the brother priests."

If his detractors considered those meetings to be evidence of Bergoglio's collaboration, the truth is that through them he was trying to "learn the identity of"—in his words—"the military chaplain who celebrated Mass" in the clandestine prisons. Once he discovered who the chaplain was, Bergoglio devised a strategy to persuade the priest-soldier "to pretend he was ill and send me in his place."

He went alone without protection and at the risk of losing face. "The generals told me that they were not aware of the situation, and they would look into it. When I found out that the priests were at ESMA, I again asked for a hearing with Videla and I let him know [where they were]." This was a clever diplomatic move because Videla must have known. And Bergoglio seemed to want to defy the leader of the junta who shortly before had assured him that he knew nothing. This led to tiring buck passing. "Videla claimed that the Army and Navy had separate commands, and that he would have to speak with Massera, but that it was not easy."

Many years have passed, but Bergoglio will never forget that evening liturgy with the dictators. "I remember that it was a Saturday afternoon. I said Mass before Videla's entire family in the residence of the commander in chief of the Army. Then I asked to speak with him— with the general—in an effort to understand where they were keeping the arrested priests."

He did not find out much, but he did not give up either. He could not. Later, the future pontiff confided to a friend that he "did some crazy things" in the months while his brother priests were held captive. "I have never been to the detention centers, except once," he told the then Argentine cardinal, "when I went with others to an Air Force base near San Miguel in the village of José C. Paz to check on the situation of a *muchacho*."

Until that dramatic afternoon of 1977.

Alicia Oliveira explains what he meant. Bergoglio's friend and lawyer at the *Centro de estudios legales sociales* (CELS) said that when Jalics and Yorio were captured, "Jorge verified that the Navy was holding them. He went to see Massera whom he told that if the priests were not released, as provincial, he would denounce what happened."

Bergoglio assured Jalics' family that he would do everything possible to free him. In a letter dated October 15, 1976 (published here for the first time), the provincial wrote: "I have taken many initiatives to secure the release of your brother, but so far I have not been successful. But I have not given up hope that he will soon be released. I have taken this situation to heart." Then he added: "The difficulties that your brother and I have had between us regarding religious life have nothing to do with the current situation. [Jalics] is a brother to me."

The "heated" exchange between Massera and Bergoglio is now reconstructed for the first time in detail.* When he saw Bergoglio, the admiral met him with a flamboyant gesture. He wanted to be seen treating the Jesuit with good humor in front of the regime's court. In reality, it was a way of mocking him in the eyes of everyone present, thinking that the priest would then never have the guts to challenge the irascible Massera.

Yet, it was not a conversation, but a verbal slugfest.

"What do you say, Bergoglio?" Such exaggerated familiarity did not please the Jesuit provincial. He was not the type for swooning—that day less than ever. "What do you say, Massera?" he countered with the same tone. The admiral, strutting around in his elegant white uniform, reacted with a frown of disappointment. Especially when the young priest planted his eyes on him and, without shifting them downward, shot it back with equal bravado.

"What do you say, Massera? I'm here to tell you that if you do not release those two priests, as provincial I will denounce this affair." The admiral did not have time

*   Based on testimonies gathered in the course of the present research and the transcripts in the *Appendix: The Questioning of Cardinal Bergoglio*, pg. 147–196]

Argentine President Isabel Perón, shown at left being honored by the military guard in 1973 while she was First Lady. After her husband Juan's death in 1974, she was elected President.

Perón served less than two years as President, in a term often marked by political and economic turmoil. By early 1976, rumblings of a military takeover began. On the night of March 23, 1976 she left the main government building in Buenos Aires via helicopter (*right*). Her flight was rerouted and she was arrested, marking the beginning of the military coup and the Dirty War that ensued.

Copyright Bettmann/Corbis / AP Images

(*Above*) Tanks and soldiers stand guard in front of the Casa Rosada, the government palace, on March 24, 1976 after President Perón was deposed by Argentina's military leaders. (*Below*) A soldier on an armored vehicle moves down a street in downtown Buenos Aires on March 25, two days after the military coup.

(*Above*) Gen. Jorge Rafael Videla, center, talks with Adm. Emilio Massera, left, and Brig. Orlando Agosti on March 17, 1976. A week later they would lead the military junta that would overthrow President Perón. In the following years, they would wage the so-called Dirty War against their political enemies, resulting in more than 9,000 people killed or "disappeared." (*Below*) Navy Captain Alfredo Astiz, aka, Gustavo Niño, aka, Rubito or the "blonde angel," was a key spy for the junta. He is seen here in 1984 on his way to an interrogation for kidnapping and murdering a teenage girl during the Dirty War.

AP Photo/Natacha Pisarenko

(*Opposite*) a young Fr. Bergoglio preaches at a Buenos Aires Church. (*Above*) The Colegio Maximo in Buenos Aires. Pope Francis studied and became a priest here. He also lived here from 1975–1986, often conspiring against the junta to provide refuge and safe passage to dozens of priests and political enemies who had been marked for elimination by the dictatorship. (*Below*) Police stand guard over a group of men detained during anti-government demonstrations in Buenos Aires on March 30, 1982. Despite being repressed, it was the largest public protest of the military dictatorship since it took power in 1976.

AP Photo/Eduardo DiBaia

AP Photo/Eduardo DiBaia

(*Above*) Hebe de Bonafini, center, the head of the Grandmothers of Plaza de Mayo, whose children "disappeared" during the Dirty War, leads one of the many marches on Buenos Aires' Plaza de Mayo in 1979. (*Below*) A man hangs photos of the "disappeared" surrounding the Plaza de Mayo monument in 2003. (*Opposite*) In 2003, members of the Argentine Forensic Anthropology Team unearth remains from a mass grave in Cordoba, one of the final resting places of many of the "disappeared."

Daniel Garcia/AFP/Getty Images

The faithful pack the square outside Buenos Aires' Metropolitan Cathedral to celebrate Pope Francis's installation. Their former bishop and fellow countryman also
is responsible for saving dozens of lives during the Dirty War.

to stammer out a reply before Bergoglio turned on his heels and walked out. The next night, the two priests, Yorio and Jalics, were drugged and loaded onto a helicopter and dumped in the middle of a swamp. They were unconscious but alive. And free.

Julio Strassera was a prosecutor in the historic trial against the military junta responsible for the dark period of desaparecidos. In short, the charges against Father Jorge are "a dirty ploy," in his judgment. "All this is completely false." He cuts it off. The Argentine legal system—as confirmed by organizations such as Amnesty International—is considered the most advanced in Latin America. The church was never let off the hook. This is demonstrated by the conviction of Christian Von Wernich, the police chaplain, for his role in killings, abductions, and torture.

CHAPTER 9

FATHER JOSÉ-LUIS CARAVIAS

"Bergoglio saved me by tricking the Secret Service"

"I was dragged into a police van and driven around for several hours. I had no idea where they were taking me, and I feared the worst. Then they opened the door, threw me out, and drove off." When they were gone, Father José-Luis Caravias realized that he was no longer in Paraguay. He was now in Clorinda—in Argentina— with no money, no identification, and no clothes. May 5, 1972 was the first day of his expulsion, and it would not be the last. Numerous ups-and-downs awaited him before he would be granted asylum in the democratically elected government of Buenos Aires.

Caravias has a broad, jovial smile and the strong hands of a farmer. You can tell by looking into his eyes that he has a number of stories to tell. The forty books he has written range from strictly theological topics to economics and sociology. He also runs a blog in which he does not shy away from saying what he thinks about the progress of Latin America—his adopted land. He retains a way of dreaming about the world he inherited from his native, sunny Andalusia [Spain] that would please even Cervantes.

"I knew the ferocity of dictatorships. I experienced it on my own skin." The Spanish Jesuit was taken in by his fellow priests in Argentina, but the situation would soon fall apart there as well. "The alarm bell was the killing of Father Mauricio Silva, the street-sweeper priest who died after deprivation and brutal torture. I realized that it was not just an [isolated] incident. I knew this because things in Paraguay had gone the same way."

* * * * *

Father Mauricio Silva, unlike Father Caravias, had not been worried. "Nobody will take someone like me seriously—someone who cleans the streets," Fr. Silva had once said. Yet, he is now one of the thirty thousand desaparecidos. His story began long ago. Born in Montevideo, he joined the Little Brothers of the Gospel—a religious congregation inspired by Charles de Foucauld*.

Before being abducted, Father Silva had worked with Bishop Angelelli in the northern part of the country, with the Salesians in Patagonia, and poor children in the landfills of Rosario. He arrived in Buenos Aires in 1970. He soon found employment as a garbage collector in the

---

*   De Foucauld was a French religious priest who lived among the nomads of the Sahara and was murdered by a gang of robbers in 1916; he was beatified by Pope Benedict XVI in 2005.

municipal district of Flores. Silva had been warned of the risks: a priest-laborer—a garbage collector moreover— would be considered a dangerous subversive. But he did not give it too much thought. On the morning of June 17, 1977, he was abducted by three men while cleaning the roads. He was forty-five years old and was swallowed up into nothingness. Little is known of him afterward— only that he was seen by several survivors in two military clandestine detention centers in very bad condition. "Father Silva was killed because he was an inconvenient witness." His elimination was a warning.

* * * * *

"Now is not the time to be heroes," Bergoglio would say some time later to the most vulnerable priests. "Yet Jalics and Yorio would not listen," Caravias continues. "Instead, he was right. As in the case of Father Silva, the death of two murdered priests would not have changed the direction of the dictatorship nor aroused the indignation of the people that could have toppled it."

Fear was stronger than the truth. Yet Father José-Luis did not learn his lesson even then. He went to the Argentine province of Chaco, slightly larger than Portugal, where farmers and ranchers did not fare much better than Paraguayan laborers. Even there, in the vast plain south of the Río Bermejo, the stubborn Jesuit founded a labor union for woodcutters who were among the most exploited and lowest paid workers. It was impossible that the landowners of twenty-six districts in the region would just stand around and do nothing. "After a

while I received death threats and began to be harassed."
It was 1973, and the Jesuits had recently elected a new
provincial: thirty-six-year-old Bergoglio.

"I am alive today, I have written forty books, I continue to promote the rights of the most vulnerable, I bring
the Gospel to the poor, in short, I am able to tell you my
story all because of him," Father Caravias articulates. As
a liberation theologian ("according to the Argentine version" he clarifies), Caravias believes the ugly attacks on
the new pope are "clearly due to international capitalism."
Father Jorge is the kind of priest who smacks of humanity. "To his accusers, a pope who denounces global poverty is too dangerous," he says.

After fourteen years as a missionary among the Indios
in Ecuador, Caravias moved to Paraguay. In the eyes of
the military there, he acted like the perfect communist.
Where the extraordinary Jesuit *misiones* had once stood,
he organized cooperatives for farmers and day-laborers.
He wanted the *campesinos* to band together in an alliance
of small producers in order to have a strong voice in the
agri-food market. Thus, they would be able to ship their
products free from the harsh conditions imposed by the
usual profiteers.

In short, Father José-Luis had a bit of a temper.
Born in 1935 in Alcalá la Real, in Andalusia, he completed his high school studies in Málaga. In 1953 at the
age of eighteen, he entered the Jesuit novitiate where he
enjoyed studying the Latin classics. Meanwhile, he had
a desire in his heart to be a missionary to the "ends of
the earth." From 1961 to 1964 he studied in Asunción,

Paraguay. Living in the land where the *reducciones* had once stood—the missions that offered dignity to the natives threatened by the *conquistadores*—was much more than an experience in one of the great Jesuit legends. After returning to Granada, Spain for four years of theology, "I had the privilege of living in a neighborhood of gypsy families." With a resume like that, it was obvious that sooner or later Father Caravias would get into trouble. Ordained a priest in 1967, he returned to Paraguay a year later. It was the era of the cultural revolutions of the 1960s and the changes of the Council. Father José-Luis felt moved—along with many others—by the springtime then blossoming in society and the Catholic Church—despite the thousand contradictions.

Once back in South America, he was no longer content with a cozy dorm room and a stack of books. So he went to work in the fields. Later as a farmer-priest he developed professional training in the agrarian leagues. But that career did not last long: "In May of 1972, I was violently abducted by the police and later abandoned in the streets of Clorinda."

In the province of Chaco in Argentina, we have already seen that things did not go much better for him. A bishop who took him in and offered him protection explained to him why. "I have here on my desk some letters that you wrote in Paraguay," explained the prelate wearing a white poncho and a crumpled *campesino* for shelter from the heat. "The problem is that what you are expressing is called Marxism." He spoke with the kindness as a spiritual father warning against heresy.

Inasmuch as he was fascinated by liberation theology and the social teachings of the Church, Caravias did not expect to be singled out as a Marxist, and he didn't worry excessively. There was a popular saying among the theologians of the younger generation: "Do not be afraid of anything, not even the Vatican."

Given the scrapes he kept getting into during his journey throughout the *Cono Sur* (Southern Cone)—from the Ecuadorian missions to Peru to Bolivia—Caravias was forced to return home in exile. At that time he did not take kindly to Father Bergoglio. Especially since Bergoglio—even though he repeatedly freed him from the clutches of the military—made sure he stayed in Spain for a while until calm returned in Buenos Aires.

"Father Bergoglio responded to my persistent requests to return to Argentina in a letter dated July 15, 1975." It was eight months before the coup, but what was about to happen was already obvious. The country was deteriorating and was about to become an open-air prison. From Chaco to Patagonia, many now understood what was to be their inescapable destiny. The international community had other things to think about—the United States had not so much as raised an eyebrow in response to the massacres perpetrated by the other Latin American regimes.

Bergoglio perfectly understood what was going on and had already begun taking precautions. In response to the pleas of Father Caravias, he sent him a mysterious letter. After the usual fraternal greetings of a distant friend, the provincial arrived at the heart of the matter:

"As regards to the possibility of your coming here, I have consulted doctors and specialists, and I must agree that this climate does not suit you, not even for a short period of time. I fear you will relapse into the illness from which you previously suffered."

Clearly, Father Provincial knew that the Secret Service was monitoring his correspondence. If the cryptic letter had been intercepted, the military would not have become suspicious. Though the Spanish Jesuit did not take it very well, he understood that the situation was worse than he imagined. The tone of the letter and the metaphor about the state of his health struck him, giving rise to questions that would have a dramatic answer the following year.

"Bergoglio was warning me that the extreme right-wing, anti-terrorism, watchdog group had decreed to eliminate me. Therefore, Spain was the 'healthiest' place for me." He was not being excessively cautious. Nor was it a convenient way to remove an unorthodox priest who made the provincial uncomfortable. "Two of my priest friends had been killed: Carlos Mujica and Mauricio Silva. Surely Bergoglio was not completely in agreement with the organizing efforts I was taking with the local people. Perhaps the numerous police reports about me had given him reason to doubt me. Nonetheless, he behaved nobly and never forced me to accept an alternative 'doctrine.' He helped me escape certain death. For this I will be forever grateful to him."

Furthermore, in that lawless province of Chaco, "I was arrested and held in jail for a night," recalls Father Caravias. "At midnight, I was subjected to a mock execution. It was a terrifying night in a filthy prison. In that moment, I came to understand the uncertainty of tomorrow not knowing if I would ever see the sunrise. Today I can say that I did well to follow the advice of Bergoglio. Both when he suggested that I leave the country, and when he explained in that letter that the climate was not suitable to me." Certainly for Father José-Luis, "as for many of us, healing has come only through much effort. It is not easy to forgive and forget those horrors. But for him, for me, and for many others, such as Father Franz Jalics, faith in Jesus was decisive [in achieving forgiveness]."

CHAPTER 10

MARTÍNEZ OSSOLA–LA CIVITA–GONZÁLEZ

*"The Martyr-Bishop Angelelli entrusted
us to him who kept us from death"*

BETWEEN June 4 and August 4, 1975, eight students were murdered in the province of La Rioja alone—in the extreme north of Argentina. The bishop, Enrique Angelelli, was also targeted by government military forces along with three young seminarians: Enrique Martínez Ossola, Miguel La Civita, and Carlos González. Angelelli was worried about the three future priests fearing they would fall victim to the *grupos* who were rounding up dissidents and purging the country from Marxist contagion. The bishop was a proponent of liberation theology and the issue of social justice was strongly felt in his northeastern diocese at the foot of the Andes.

To this day there are still few alternatives to working either in a factory or in the backbreaking countryside in the district of La Rioja. In those parts working as a labor unionist or demanding better working conditions would put you on the black list as a subversive. In this cluster of neighborhoods with a population of less than two hundred thousand people, politics is more than a local matter. For some quirk of fate, this semi-desert region has given rise to two presidents: Isabelita Perón (the second wife of the "re-founder" of Argentina, Juan), and Carlos Menem, the charismatic and controversial head of state twice elected to the Casa Rosada between 1989 and 1999. The principal town of La Rioja is 930 miles from Buenos Aires. Yet, the distance is not only geographic. If it were not for *telenovelas* (soap operas) and Argentine cuisine, there would be little in common between the people of the nation's capital and those of the Sierras.

Angelelli and Bergoglio had different perspectives in theology and, consequently, pastoral work. Both, however, held one another in high esteem. Angelelli was not the type of person to accept compromises particularly in his strong support of the *campesinos* in his diocese and in his fight against the exploitation of the farmhands whose situation was more akin to slavery. For these reasons, he was targeted by the regime. However, they offered him a way out by asking him to celebrate Mass in the barracks where they tortured dissidents. But he said no. And he also refused to appear on stage next to General President Videla, for the simple reason that "the bishop cannot shake the hand of someone who oppresses his people." A man like this would never have allowed his seminarians to fall into the hands of the torturers. So when he decided to move them to safety, the bishop asked Provincial Bergoglio to personally look after them. And so they were received into the residence of San Miguel in Buenos Aires.

None of them knew Bergoglio. When they arrived at the college, they thought they would be greeted by a secretary or someone who would then lead them to Fr. Bergoglio in his office. Instead, a rather young Jesuit met them as soon as they entered. "Welcome, I am Father Jorge. You must be the ones from La Rioja."

"Yes, here we are. Where are you from?" they asked, showing they did not understand who he was.

"I am the Father Provincial." They almost fainted from embarrassment.

"He was the highest authority of the Jesuits in Argentina, and he introduced himself as an average Joe," they recall today.

In fact, Angelelli had not told the seminarians the true reason why he had transferred them to the province of Buenos Aires. "We thought he had sent us there to finish our studies," explained La Civita. In fact he had brought them to safety and rescued them from the purges of the regime. In the eyes of the military, the three young men of La Rioja bore a double original sin: they loved serving in the poorest villages, but worse they fully shared in the values of their bishop.

* * * * *

Enrique Angelelli was born in Córdoba in 1923 to a family of Italian immigrants. In 1961, when he was only thirty-eight years old, Pope John XXIII appointed him auxiliary bishop of Córdoba. The following year, he participated in the sessions of the Second Vatican Council, embracing the spirit of renewal that would eventually earn him the enmity of the Argentine military. In 1964, he was appointed bishop of La Rioja. He introduced himself to the community saying: "I do not come to be served, but to serve all without distinction, without regard for social class or way of thinking and believing. Like Jesus, I want to be a servant of our poor brothers and sisters."

On August 4, 1976, the bishop was returning home from the town of Chamical. Fr. Arturo Aldo Pinto was driving as they traveled along the dusty potholed roads. The landscape along that stretch is rich in scenery. The switchbacks wrapping around the Sierras open up to a beautiful view of the Andes in the distance. Along the more than 620 miles separating La Rioja from the nation's capital is an expanse of fields, swamps, and large herds of cattle. The bishop's Fiat 125 Multicarga pick-up was traveling along one of those high mountain roads.

The mood inside the vehicle was not good. Angelelli had just met with the people of Chamical who were feeling afraid and unsettled. He went to console them, but his visit was not limited to prayers of encouragement. He had managed to gather intelligence regarding the death of two priests, Fathers Gabriel Longueville and Carlos de Dios Murias, who were murdered fifteen days earlier. The dossier contained proof of the culprits' guilt.

While traveling around a canyon, Angelelli's car was suddenly flanked by a Peugeot 404. Unexpectedly, the overtaking vehicle nudged the Fiat sending it down into the ravine. Angelelli died on impact. Father Arturo Pinto was unconscious leading the killers to believe they had completed their job. It had to look like an accident.

Father Pinto managed to escape and somehow find the courage to report the incident; the case was archived by the police on the same day. But his protests went nowhere. No documents were found in the wreckage of the Fiat. The binder containing the information on elimination of the two priests had disappeared. During one of General Videla's trials some twenty years later, a witness would testify that the entire dossier was seen in the Minister of the Interior's office a few days after Angelelli's assassination:

> A confidential report dated May, 1978 prepared by English spies shows that Monsignor Achille Silvestrini, vicar Secretary of State of the Holy See, told a British diplomat that the Argentine government was incapable of providing detailed answers on the issue of human rights. It limited itself to the publication of lists of those imprisoned or who had disappeared.

This discovery was made by historian, Giuseppe Casarrubea. The documentation was discovered during one of several investigations on the role of Anglo-Americans in Italian politics at the end of the Second World War.

Silvestrini revealed an unreleased fact—that the Vatican had suspected from the beginning that what happened to the bishop of La Rioja was not an accident. "The Holy See is convinced that Argentine Bishop Angelelli was murdered." As reported in the British documents, "His car collided with a truck while returning from the funeral of three priests who had been killed by the police."

According to the Córdoba Tribunal in its ruling in 2008, "the murder of Bishop Angelelli was part of a systematic plan of elimination of people carried out by security forces and the Armed Forces who controlled the government of Argentina."

The president at that time, Néstor Kirchner, declared the day of the killing of Angelelli to be a day of national mourning. But until 2006, the church had never officially ruled on the fate of the bishop. Three decades had passed since the day of the phony accident. The archbishop of Buenos Aires, Jorge Bergoglio, commemorated his old friend during a Mass in La Rioja at which all the country's bishops were present, saying: "He shed his blood to preach the Gospel. Angelelli was a man of encounter, of the margins, in love with his people."

Bergoglio also referred to the priests, Gabriel Longueville and Carlos de Dios Murias, and the layman, Wenceslao Pedernera, who were murdered in La Rioja shortly before Angelelli. Bishop Angelelli had just collected information about their fate incriminating the generals' government.

* * * * *

Bergoglio was in Peru on the day in which the prelate was driven into the ravine. As soon as he received the news, he returned to San Miguel. Martínez Ossola, La Civita, and

González were distraught with pain and terrified at what might happen next. They had not yet finished mourning their bishop when they heard quick heavy footsteps coming down the hallway around 2:00 a.m. They trembled with fear. There was a curfew then and no one made that kind of noise at night except for soldiers. They realized the footsteps were headed toward their room.

"It is Jorge," Bergoglio whispered from the other side of the door. He entered the room, embraced them, and tried to console them. Given what had happened, there was no time for tears. This time the provincial was firm. The way he spoke, the tone of his voice, and his conversation led the three to understand the real reason they had been sent away from Angelelli. "You must never separate from one another," Father Jorge ordered them. "Stay together and move cautiously. If you are together, it will be harder for them to arrest the three of you at the same time."

They never thought they would end up in a situation like that. In the darkness of the Argentine night, they felt like Christians in the era of the catacombs. They knew they were in danger, but the fatherly demeanor of Bergoglio reassured them. "We knew we were in good hands," they recounted many years later.

Father Provincial carefully instructed the three young men. "Among other things, he said that we should never go out after dusk, and he recommended we remain cautious even within the college." No place could be considered truly safe. "Don't use the main staircase and make yourself as inconspicuous as possible. When you need to go to your rooms or access other parts of the college, use the elevator." Communications were another vulnerable point. Therefore, he cautioned that phone calls should be reduced to a minimum, preferably using cryptic language but without inducing suspicion. Using weather metaphors or state of health was a good way to make themselves understood, Bergoglio advised.

Additionally, they were to avoid sending mail from the San Miguel post office. Instead, he told them to give it to trustworthy people who would then bring it to outlying post offices. There, censors would be more lax and correspondence would be more difficult to trace back to the Jesuits of the Colegio Máximo.

During those three months, they witnessed Father Jorge committed to obtaining the release of Fathers Yorio and Jalics. "We saw how he strove to help them; he remained behind the scenes to work out a solution. He managed to save them although it took a long time to realize that both owe their lives to Bergoglio."

During their stay in San Miguel, Father La Civita reports, "we realized that Bergoglio allowed people to take refuge in the college under the pretext of making spiritual exercises. From there, people fled abroad with new documents." Could he have done more? "He was the provincial superior of the Jesuits, not Superman. As far as I know, he did everything he could. Even more."

Since then, Bergoglio never forgot about the three young men. In 1978, when the situation had calmed down for the three, the seminarians returned to La Rioja. Father Jorge went there. "He came for our priestly ordination and led us in the spiritual exercises. But this time it was not a pretext. Bergoglio, as always, took this commitment seriously. Sometimes too much."

The heat was terrible in La Rioja. "The three of us decided to jump into a river to cool off." What happened next will forever remain etched in their memory. A lesson Bergoglio style: "Good, no problem," said the unabashed provincial. "He put on his swimming suit, got into the water, and gave us the retreat in the stream."

Father Quique, one of the three seminarians "saved": "The secrets of San Miguel"

More so than the verdicts against the dictators, proof of their defeat is manifest in the cheerful face of Enrique Martínez Ossola. Known as "Father Quique," he is pastor of the Annunciation of the Lord in La Rioja.

Father Quique returned home to La Rioja after having been driven out by the military junta. The events of that time have since strengthened his convictions, rather than diminish them. "The preferential option for the poor is not negotiable. And with Bergoglio in Rome, we can never go back," he says.

His testimony confirms what the others said. "In 1975, as a seminarian in the diocese of La Rioja, I traveled with Miguel La Civita and Carlos González to the town of San Miguel in the province of Buenos Aires. Our bishop, Enrique Angelelli, was with us."

That group must have seemed like a gaggle of troublemakers to the official hierarchy. They did not have the ways of sophisticated city people appearing instead as unambitious students. It seemed they did not aspire to be anything more than simple priests ministering to the marginalized of society.

"After several attempts at finding lodging in the capital city or nearby, the bishop and superiors of the University of San José decided we would live in the Jesuit College and take the necessary theology courses for our priestly ordination." Bergoglio did not hesitate to appease Angelelli. Father Quique continued:

> In the college, we were met by a young priest who was very friendly. He was the provincial superior, the highest authority of the Jesuit order in all of Argentina, but in the beginning we did not realize this. Right away, he sensed our apprehension and created an informal and fraternal relationship with us. He and his brother priests allowed us the greatest freedom. They did not even impose fixed timetables on us for lunch and dinner. We could come and go based on the time we had available.

The informal atmosphere contrasted with the imposing austerity of the place: large windows, long corridors, shelves full of books, and polished marble. "Often we shared a meal together with the future pope in a family environment," recalls Quique Martinez. "For us, there was no better place to take on our studies."

Their fears were not unfounded. "On March 24, 1976, we were in class studying when the military coup took place." Although the news was censored by the military, it was nonetheless dramatic. "Shortly after, we learned that the house where we had lived in La Rioja had been ransacked, and many of the books we had studied were confiscated."

They continued receiving discouraging news from La Rioja. "Priests and lay people were arrested for no apparent reason. They were trying to isolate Bishop Angelelli. He was the object of all the interrogations."

In his vast province, the closest church for some people was dozens of miles away and many people could not come to Sunday Mass. Thus, the liturgy presided over by Angelelli in his cathedral was transmitted via live radio. "One of the first things the military did was refuse to authorize further transmissions. Instead, the Mass transmitted on radio would be celebrated by a military chaplain. In short, the situation was deteriorating irreparably. Their sole purpose was to foster a climate of suspicion and persecution," says Father Martínez.

Meanwhile, people in Buenos Aires were beginning to learn of the first arrests and disappearances—of people "sucked up" into nothingness. "It became an everyday occurrence. In June of that same year, two seminarians of the Assumptionist Congregation—Rodríguez and Di Pietro—were abducted in the crowded district of La Manuelita. We shared the same theological vision with them. Thus, an era of terror was established in the country. It did not spare anyone: students, workers, labor unionists, professionals, catechists. Any activity relating to social action was considered suspect in the eyes of the military authorities."

On July 4, 1976, a fellow student at the Colegio
Máximo, Emilio Barletti, fell victim to the "massacre of
the Pallotine Fathers." The police were convinced that
the priests of the parish of *San Patricio* were working in
connection with another group that carried out its activities in a parish in the slums of Bajo Flores. A few weeks
earlier, a military raid there had done away with some
activists, including Sister Mónica Quinteiro and a student, Mónica María Candelaria Mignone, who was the
daughter of one of the main defenders of human rights in
Argentina, Emilio Fermín Mignone. They were accused
of complicity with guerrilla groups—the same charge
that the authorities now lodged against the Pallotine
fathers of St. Patrick's.

The massacre took place in the dead of the cold
Argentine winter around 2:00 a.m. on Sunday, July 4. The
church of St. Patrick's is located in the neighborhood of
Belgrano, a good middle-class enclave of Buenos Aires. A
black Peugeot sedan stopped in front of the rectory where
the priests lived. A police car was already parked nearby.
The two cars communicated by flashing their headlights
when the officers put their car in reverse and left the area.
According to some witnesses who observed the scene
from their window, everything happened in sync. Others
maintained that the patrol car was there unrelatedly and
arrived only after General Martínez—who lived in the
area—had called the police fearing an act of terrorism.

Once the patrol car left, the *patota* gang went to work.
Four men got out. When one of the Pallotine priests
opened the door, the men pushed him inside threatening

with their machine guns. They then woke up the other four priests whom they insulted and beat. They forced them to get on their knees and then they executed them. The bodies of Fathers Leaden, Dufau, and Kelly in addition to seminarians, Barbeito and Barletti, were found lined up on the ground in a huge puddle of blood.

Fourteen days later on July 18, the priests Gabriel Longueville and Carlos Murias were executed in Chamical in the province of La Rioja. One week later, the layperson Wenceslaus Pederson executed in the Department of Sanagasta. As has been said, Bishop Angelelli was later killed while investigating these murders.

"From that moment onward, Father Jorge paid special attention to us," says Father Quique today. "He did everything possible to help us through this difficult time." Father Quique and his two companions at San Miguel, too, felt compelled to help Father Provincial. Even if the other Jesuits did not know the real reason they were staying in San Miguel, Quique and the other two seminarians now knew why Angelelli wanted them under Bergoglio's care: so they would not end up like Fathers Leaden, Dufau, and Kelly, seminarians Barletti and Barbeito, and the others.

Quietly and with utmost secrecy, "we worked with Bergoglio to help those who were introduced as university students or as young people there for a retreat. We knew that the real reason they were there was to escape persecution." How many were there? "During the period we stayed in San Miguel, we dealt with about twenty people."

Shortly after Bergoglio's election to the papacy, Father Martínez wrote a letter to "Papa Jorge." Their relationship had always remained strong. Quique regularly kept him updated throughout his vocational journey [as a seminarian] and later on with his pastoral work as a priest. Even though Bergoglio was now the pope in Rome, Father Quique kept him informed of what he was doing in La Rioja. And Bergoglio has remained interested, responding to at least one of the priest's letters even after becoming Pope Francis:

Dear Quique, today I received your letter dated May 1. It gave me much joy. Your story of the patron feast celebration brought me a breath of fresh air. I am fine here, and I have not lost my peace in the wake of a totally surprising event [election to the papacy] which I believe is a gift from God. I try to maintain the same way of being and acting as when I was in Buenos Aires. If I were to change at my age, I would seem ridiculous. I did not want to live in the Apostolic palace. I go there for work and audiences [or 'meetings']. I have remained at Casa Santa Marta, the residence that hosted us during the conclave and that receives bishops, priests, and laypersons. I am visible to the people and I have a normal life: public Mass in the morning, I eat in the dining hall with the others, et cetera. All this is very good for me and prevents me from becoming isolated.

[...]

I ask you the favor of praying for me and asking others to pray for me. Greetings to Carlos and

Miguel. May Jesus bless you and the Holy Virgin look after you.

—Fraternally, Francisco.

Thanks be to God, "Jorge is not at all changed," according to Father Quique. The priest takes heart and recognizes in the pope's letter the spirit of the silent hero from forty years earlier.

Father Quique's reconstruction of those events has several confirmations: some from other religious priests, some from diocesan clergy who had contact with the Jesuits then. Among them are José Luis Vendramin, Carlos Gonzáles, and Vicente Ramos. At different times, they referred to the protection they received from Father Bergoglio and during periods of "spiritual exercises" in the College of San Miguel they witnessed the comings and goings of other young people who found themselves in the government's crosshairs.

Father Vendramin is now pastor of a church in the diocese of San Miguel not far from the Jesuit College. In an interview given on March 28, 2013 to *L'Osservatore Romano*, he recalled those years and how he learned of the risks that Enrique Martínez and Miguel La Civita were facing.

> I was here in [the city of] José Clemente Paz, but I attended the seminary of San Miguel where the two lived and also where Bergoglio was [provincial]. What we experienced during that period was very difficult. People who are not from Argentina have no idea what this era was like for us. Priests risked great dangers

because they were among the few who spoke of freedom in a time when freedom did not exist.

Not only that: "I was also there with three other seminarians. And I advised them to be careful, especially when the soldiers were seen near the college."

CHAPTER 11

SERGIO AND ANA GOBULIN

"We owe our lives to him"

"THEY smashed doors and threw things about. They said they were looking for weapons." They did not care that there was a little girl or that this family had erred only in fighting for the rights and the dignity of the marginalized. It was an intimidation.

The secret police did not like the idea of "liberation" that was then penetrating every corner of society and various institutions: in the Church, now open to the world—experiences and people came together that never would—have happened in an earlier age; in labor unions; in university departments; and in neighborhoods throughout all of Argentina.

The voices of Sergio and Ana Gobulin betray the emotion of those forced to untangle the barbed wire of their memories to make sense of what happened. "Contrary to what some would have you believe, Bergoglio was part of this climate of freshness. He had his feet firmly planted in the tradition of Christian values, but his vision gazed forward—farther than we could imagine," says Sergio.

It was through that healthy realism of his that Father Jorge convinced them that if they were dead, he and his wife could not continue their mission. They speak about what happened without regret. For thirty years now they have been living in Italy after a daring escape from Buenos Aires. It was not easy to settle in Friuli [Northern Italy]—the same place Sergio had emigrated from with his parents when he was a child unconscious of what would become of his life in a distant land full of hope.

Now that he is almost in his 70s, Gobulin carefully chooses his words and memories as one does who wants to place on the scales of life only that which has weight. "Inspired by post-conciliar momentum, I decided to leave the province of Santa Fe to study theology in the nation's capital." They also accepted laypersons in the college of the Jesuits in San Miguel. Sergio continues:

> In 1970, while still a student of theology I decided to live in a *villa miseria* [author's note: shanty town] on the outskirts of Buenos Aires in consistency with my beliefs. With a growing group of neighborhood residents, we engaged in different works: assistance to poor families from Argentina or neighboring countries, the creation of a night school for adult literacy, health care, assistance to single mothers and other works with social value.

These were the years of hope in the building of a more just society. This, recalls Gobulin, "entailed a preferential option for the marginalized." For him it meant, first of all, being among them.

It was during this period in which he met Bergoglio, who was not yet a priest. He would be ordained on December 13, 1969 four days before his thirty-third birthday. Meanwhile, Sergio earned a living by working as a clerk in one of the Jesuit research centers. There he would meet his future wife, Ana, who assisted with the children of some teachers.

From then onward, the friendship between Father Jorge and Gobulin would travel thousands of miles. Sergio had the opportunity to accompany the future pontiff during his travels by car throughout the country. Among the endless expanses of the *pampas* or while traveling through the neglected slums, "not only did they speak of the mission of the Church, the obligation of Christians, but also of the situation in Argentina—of change, hope, and difficulty."

In the villa miseria, Sergio lent a helping hand looking for materials to build houses, tidying up the streets, helping families recover after floods, digging ditches, and building a network for drinking water and other facilities for the community. This led to a school that taught reading, a clinic for basic medical care, and a center to help unwed mothers.

"In the midst of great difficulties," Sergio recalls, "there was an atmosphere of joy among the people. We organized parties and dances in the evenings to raise funds necessary to purchase the materials. Most of the people of the 'villa' attended them. We laughed among ourselves when we spoke of 'raising money from people who didn't have any.'"

"The years of dictatorship were a period of total denial of all freedom of thought, expression, information, and action," remembers Gobulin. "They were years of harsh repression against those who opposed the junta. Many of us, especially young people, reacted. We were convinced of the need to fight against the denial of the fundamental rights of the person. We acted through our everyday actions day after day. And for this reason, many people—more than thirty thousand—disappeared into the dark tunnels without ever returning."

The distance was short from the ABCs to political vindication. People were beginning to make themselves heard in the villa miseria. They asked to no longer be treated as third-class citizens. Once he was appointed provincial of the Jesuits, Bergoglio wanted to know about those situations first hand. "The first time he stayed with us for a few days. He returned to the college deeply impressed by that experience."

Sergio and Ana were married on November 14, 1975. Father Jorge presided over their wedding celebration in a parish in the district. Also present were the parents of the bride and groom who for years carefully hid photos of the wedding, for them a precious memory that they did not want to fall into the hands of the police.

A few days after exchanging vows, their house was ransacked by soldiers while the newlyweds were at the movies. When they returned, it looked as if a tank had ploughed through. "We had not done anything wrong, we did not possess weapons, we did not belong to any terrorist organization," says Sergio.

Sergio and his wife cleaned up the house with the help of neighbors from the district. They continued on as if nothing had happened. They believed that the officers had concluded that their work among the poor did not mask ulterior motives.

Almost a year later, on October 11, 1976, Sergio Gobulin became *chupado*. That morning he had taken the day off work to settle some family matters. Ana, too, stayed at home; in another twenty-four hours, her maternity leave was set to expire.

The dissident hunters displayed a level of amateurism that day and their operation almost failed. When they discovered that Sergio was not in his office, they went looking for him in the neighborhood. Then they came across him along the road, not far from the shack he lived in.

After a flurry of punches, they threw a burlap sack over his head and tied his hands behind his back. They took him away without giving him time to react. Ana's colleagues, however, had time to warn her. Men of unmistakable repute came to the school where she taught. She had managed to hide among some acquaintances, thereby escaping the worst. But not Sergio. For eighteen days, he was at the mercy of strange men who transferred him various times: prisons, private homes, barracks, prisons again. The questions were always the same: "What do you do in the neighborhood? Who is part of your terrorist group?"

They went looking for Ana at her parents' house. There were no weapons. No suspicious documents. Nothing at all. "So what do you want?" her mother asked. "Those who have weapons in their heads," they answered.

As soon as Father Jorge found out what happened, he launched a rescue mission in two directions: extract Sergio from the soldiers and also keep Ana safe. As usual, the Jesuit began to investigate on his own. He asked questions and looked around. He went to the police in support of his friends. After the usual ups and downs, he managed to free Sergio.

Gobulin recounts, "The eighteen days of my abduction were truly harsh, both due to physical tortures as well as psychological ones. After my release, my family members told me of the efforts that Father Jorge and the then Vice-Consul of Italy in Argentina, Enrico Calamai, made for my search and rescue."

Sergio lost track of time a thousand times during that period, and he feared the end was near. He was sure October 29 was his last day. They gave him a beating, one of many. In reality, the tormentors were letting him go and this was their "*adios.*" In three weeks, he had never been able to see their face. He was dumped in the street still tied and blindfolded not far from his in-laws' house. He was in so much pain he could not even stand up.

There wasn't much time. Through the Apostolic Nunciature, Bergoglio involved the Italian consul Enrico Calamai—the hero responsible for hundreds of rescues.

"After my liberation, Calamai had me admitted to the Italian Hospital of Buenos Aires together with my wife and daughter for security reasons. Ana and I thought we would move away from the capital once my health recovered."

They stayed in the ward for more than a month. One day they told Fr. Jorge about their plan to stay in Argentina but move inland. They would be far from the military and they believed they would be able to start over. However, Fr. Jorge said, "Now is the time to be courageous. Your troubles are not over for you, not for Argentina. They will look for you again. Listen to me, you must leave the country." Sergio Gobulin recalls: "He told us about various attempts he made to obtain my release and prove my innocence. This required him to meet with several high ranking officers in the Armed Forces. This is why we had to leave: he found out that other groups in the army were looking for me."

"When my health permitted, Dr. Calamai accompanied us to the proper offices to obtain the necessary documents to denounce the incident," Gobulin remembers. "He urged me to do so, saying that it would be helpful to the Italian government in documenting cases of abductions and the disappearance of its citizens."

After contacting him to verify the account, Calamai explained that he "never dealt directly with Bergoglio. In fact, throughout those years I never heard his name." However, from the nunciature "I received lists, and it is possible that Gobulin was among them." Sergio and his wife recount how they received a brand new passport directly from the Italian Consulate and three one-way tickets to Italy.

Calamai accompanied them to fill out the expatriation documents: "He even waited on line with us. There was the possibility I would be kidnapped again, but the risk was much lower in the presence of a diplomat," recalls Sergio with all the gratitude one owes a hero like him, who was able to save hundreds of lives by providing safe passage to anyone who asked. A man like this would have deserved, at minimum, a promotion to a higher rank or even a seat as life senator. Instead, he missed out on his career.

Jorge Bergoglio, too, had to pay a price to the professional slanderers. And this is the only reason why Sergio and Ana chose to break the covenant of silence that lasted almost forty years. They never wanted to tell anyone their story. But now they say: "Far from entering into the controversy about Bergoglio's actions during the dictatorship; far from taking sides pro or con, our intent is to make our testimony during that period public—not just private. We believe it goes beyond the figure of Bergoglio." Sergio and Ana clarify what they mean: "We are not interested in personal publicity or taking advantage of our friendship with Father Jorge. The man to whom we owe our life has become pope. And we who have known him intimately cannot help but see the hand of Providence."

The torturers who drowned tens of thousands of dissidents in the waters of the Río de la Plata did not understand subtleties. Their reasoning did not allow alternatives: living among the poor equated to "communism." Sergio and Ana understood politics as a commitment, solidarity, and defense of the weak. But that was not enough.

"I remember when Jorge came into my hovel made of sheet metal and earthen floor," recalls Sergio. "He stopped in for a few days for spiritual retreat. During those moments, you could tell he was not the type of person to just chat about theology cooling off with a fan. He was a man with a mission. He listened to the poor and watched them in their misery and their impulses. He immersed himself in their world and in their suffering. He went down into the depths of their hearts in order to then take them back up with his message of hope."

Father Jorge talked with very few people about these visits to the slums. "We lived during a great period of transformation. We were part of a community that was finally experiencing renewal. There was an excitement that we will never be able to forget," recall the spouses. In July 2013, they visited Aparecida, Brazil as pilgrims during World Youth Day and once again embraced their friend who had become *Papa Francisco*.

Sergio repeats what he does not want people to forget: "I was fortunate to get out alive. But it was due to the insistence of important people who came in search of me in the torturous barracks. It is in here where the figure of Bergoglio emerges."

Returning to the Southern Cone is a heart-filled experience every time for them. It is impossible to erase what happened on January 17, 1977. They arrived on the dock of Buenos Aires together with Father Jorge. He watched the ship sail away in the reflection of the summer sunset. Twenty-seven years earlier, his parents had arrived in Argentina on one of those ships. Sergio, was with them and he, too, arrived in the "new world" when he was a child of just four years old. "Once we set sail, we realized that Father Jorge had saved our life. He also gave us money to cover the cost of expatriation. If it hadn't been for him, we would not be here to talk about it."

Life sometimes defines itself in a single moment. The grisly account of wrecked lives, of great dreams suddenly vanished, would be even crueler if it were not for people like Bergoglio. "In addition to 'liberating' people who were missing, or others who were in danger of disappearing, Father Jorge 'indirectly' saved many others. This statement," observes Sergio Gobulin "is not verifiable with logic; rather, it is a conviction I came to realize after my release." It is an argument that goes far. "In order to execute their repressive plans, the military dictatorship sought to acquire 'names' from their victims in addition to stories and facts. They sought to extract the names of friends, co-workers, and neighbors. They used physical or psychological torture, and even drugged victims to do so. This created further disappearances."

The degree of resistance varied from one person to the next. There were some who spilled their guts at the mere sight of the "irons," and there were those who gave in only after being mutilated. "It is clear that the more time one was tortured, the more their limits of endurance yielded." For this reason, many people were saved "unbeknownst to them" by the commitment of Bergoglio.

"As was my case, since he was able to reduce by weeks, if not months, time spent in the hands of the torturers, it is very likely that fewer names were mentioned. Thus, dozens of people were never abducted by the military only because they did not have time or the opportunity to extract the 'suspicious incidents' concerning them," says Sergio.

Father Jorge never stopped calling Sergio and Ana. Six months after they set sail to Italy, Bergoglio wanted to personally see how the Gobulins had settled. So he went to visit them in Friuli.

One year earlier there had been a devastating earthquake in Italy's northeastern regions. And shortly after Bergoglio arrived, there was another small quake in the middle of the night. "I took our daughter and ran out of the house while Sergio woke up Jorge," recalls Ana. No one in the crowded street knew that the guest of the Gobulins was a priest. Still terrified from the devastation of the previous year, the people started to pray in the dark and they asked for the protection of the Creator. Father Bergoglio was deeply moved by their devotion. The next morning he asked to be accompanied through the streets to get to know the faithful and devoted townspeople more personally. "We saw some of them. After normalcy returned, instead of praying, however they were now swearing." Bergoglio did not lose his composure, however. Instead, he remained silent and prayed for them.

Some years later, when the Gobulin family had another opportunity to meet their priest friend from Buenos Aires, he remembered that short stay in Friuli.

Then suddenly, with that sly expression that preceded a witty remark he asked, "Let me ask you this, in your town do people still pray in that way?"

There are many things that Sergio and Ana will never forget about Father Jorge. For example, in 1978 just six months after they left Argentina, the provincial went to see Sergio's mother who had remained in the country with the rest of her family. He gave her an envelope. Inside was some money for a trip and a note that said, "Go and visit your son."

CHAPTER 12

JOSÉ MANUEL DE LA SOTA

"Everyone knows he saved dozens of lives"

"*TE queremos papa Francisco! Llenas de alegría nuestros corazones*" (We love you Pope Francis! Our hearts are filled with joy!). Some saw typical political opportunism in this tweet by the governor of Córdoba a few minutes after the election of Pope Francis. José Manuel de la Sota is a member of the Argentine Justicialist Party, but in 2011 he had founded a Federal Peronist faction with other governors of the provinces in opposition to Kirchnerism.

Yet, his enthusiasm is sincere. In fact, De la Sota is beholden to Bergoglio with a debt that cannot be repaid, "He saved my life by getting me out of prison."

There is an affection that has existed between Córdoba and the Jesuits for many centuries. The Jesuit Block and the Estancias of Córdoba (*Manzana Jesuítica y Las Estancias de Córdoba*) are part of an ex-mission built long ago by the Jesuit order. In the year 2000, the site was declared a UNESCO World Heritage Site by the United Nations. The *Manzana Jesuítica*, in the city center, contains the headquarters of the University of Córdoba (one of the oldest in South America), Monserrat Secondary School, a church, and other buildings admired by thousands of tourists every year. The complex, whose foundation dates back to 1615, was abandoned by the Jesuits in 1767 when King Charles III of Spain ordered their expulsion from the subcontinent. The Jesuit site was then taken over by the Franciscans who gave it back to them in 1853 when the Jesuits were able to return to the Americas.

The importance of the role of the Jesuit missions in the province of Córdoba is highlighted by a fact: the road of the *Estancias*—which connected buildings, houses and chapels built by the Jesuit Society of Jesus—is about 155 miles long.

This is the geography of the soul in which De la Sota grew up. He attended high school in Córdoba at the Institute of the Immaculate before graduating with a degree in law and beginning a career as a lawyer.

Already in the early 1970s, the future governor (who for a short period also served as Ambassador of Argentina in Brazil) had a run-in with the police after being prosecuted for "Peronist proselytism." The coup d'état of 1976 stopped the clock of history and the calendar of millions of people.

"Father Jorge intervened repeatedly after my family told him what happened to me." Young José Manuel was abducted after a political rally in Villa Cura Brochero, a town in the province of Córdoba. "Bergoglio was able to intercede after I was arrested by the military. He intervened many times to secure my release," recalled the politician. And De la Sota also speaks of witnessing other rescues: "Many of us received his charitable help in the difficult moments experienced during the military dictatorship," he states.

"I come from a Catholic family," he recalled, describing his childhood education. "Many priests, and even bishops, at that time did a lot of good and risking many dangers in the process. Bergoglio was one of them, and anyone who attacks him is a coward because everyone knows what he did to save dozens of lives."

De la Sota will not say any more about this—at least for now. In fact, he does not wish to stir up controversy. Nor does he wish to appear like so many people who have already rewritten their resume highlighting their close friendship with the pope. "I think that Argentina is going through a very special moment right now. A neighborhood priest has become pope, and he is showing all of us that he is genuinely humble, indicating the pathway to conceive and build a new humanity."

This is one thing, however, that De la Sota must say. At the risk of creating enmity even within his own party, he stresses one sentence: "The few who speak maliciously about the pope should be ashamed."

CHAPTER 13

JUAN CARLOS SCANNONE

*"This is the first time I have said this:
he stopped a raid against me"*

PART Two concludes by returning to the long initial conversation with the theologian, Juan Carlos Scannone. At just over eighty years old, he is the greatest exponent of what has been known as the *teología del pueblo* (theology of the people) since the eighties. The Jesuit priest has some things in common with liberation theologians such as the drive for social justice and the call for an economy based on ethics "in accordance with the social doctrine of the church," he specifies. As for the rest, there are few significant similarities. The military, however, could not make such subtle distinctions. *Pueblo* (people) or not, they were all "communist priests."

Today Scannone is the director of the Institute of Philosophical Studies within the department of Theology and Philosophy in San Miguel where Bergoglio was rector between 1980 and 1986. The remarkable memory of Father Juan Carlos allows him to take a long journey back into the history of Argentina, from the twilight of the dictatorship to the rebirth of democracy. In an effort to direct the conversation toward his extraordinary story as a man of faith, I ask him, "Even though you are considered the leading exponent of a movement so opposed by the military junta, why has there never been any news of persecution against you?"

"Because I never spoke about it! Many years had passed, and I did not want to create debate and controversy regarding Archbishop Bergoglio. But now that my friend Jorge has become Papa Francisco, I can tell you that yes, he covered my back and saved me. And he did so in a variety of ways."

Before returning to this topic, Scannone wanted to recall how he met the future pope:

> He was a student of mine of Greek and literature. In time, the roles were reversed and Father Jorge became first my spiritual father, then my rector, and finally my provincial. It is natural, therefore, that we were close. He has always been very austere—a man of great intelligence even in practical things. For example, he drives well. When he was rector, he decided not to have a driver. He did the same thing when he became archbishop. He can do many things at the same time. In our region, people like him are called "orchestra men" in the sense that they are capable of playing different instruments.

In an interview with the *L'Osservatore Romano*, Scannone recalled that Bergoglio once "typed up an article, did the laundry, and then received someone for spiritual direction." He was also good in the kitchen. They still remember a stuffed piglet dish of his called "à la Bergoglio" in the college.

As mentioned above, the dictatorship perceived the "theology of the people" as a threat despite its substantial difference from so-called Marxist theologians. Without distinction they persecuted and brutalized priests, laity, catechists, and nuns who worked in the villas miseria and the slums. "The military was incapable of distinguishing subtleties," explains Scannone. For them, to speak of liberation or of a preferential option for the poor meant only one word: *comunismo*. Personally, I have never had anything to do with Marxism, yet they still considered me a communist. Even the future Cardinal Eduardo Francisco Pironio, for whom the cause of beatification is currently underway, was believed by the Secret Services to be a senior leader of the "Red Church."

But what did Scannone advocate specifically regarding liberation theology? "The difference," responds Father Juan Carlos "is that here in Argentina neither the Marxist methodology of the analysis of reality nor other categories imported from Marxism were ever used. On the contrary, we still promote an appreciation of culture and popular religion. Hence the definition of a teología del pueblo (theology of the people). The people, therefore, become the bearer of cultural values which nourish the enculturation of the faith through popular religiosity.

And this happens as much for the faithful as for the entire Latin American people. In short, this theological movement prefers the historical-cultural analysis instead of social-structural typical of liberation theology."

Scannone then tells how the regime kept an eye on him, his colleagues, and his brother priests.

> The police often wandered around here, and certainly not because they were concerned about the security of the college. They raided the building at night—it must have been the end of '77. They came through the gate and surrounded the building with their trucks in what was a real raid. I still remember the sound of their footsteps in the hallways. It was dark and I could not tell how many there were. But by the noise made by their leather boots, I would guess there were at least twenty in addition to others who were outside. We were very scared. From the way they burst in, I feared the army had been ordered to carry out a roundup and I felt I was their target.

Why him?

> Because I was considered an exponent of liberation theology, a movement the regime believed was a smokescreen [for communism]. Bergoglio made me realize I was at risk in many ways. While our positions were theologically different—though I would say not so

distant—he never wanted me to be silenced. Not even when several bishops intervened with Father Provincial trying to convince him that my positions made them uncomfortable, or were even disreputable. But Father Jorge never asked me to change my views. On the contrary, he helped me get my ideas outside Argentina by bypassing the military censorship.

How did Bergoglio react during the raid?

As a charismatic leader. He encouraged us and calmed each one of us. He ordered the military to leave. They had no right to be there especially in that manner. He knew they would not go away, but he presented himself firmly in order to gain respect. He knew there was nothing to find in the college. He spoke to them directly, but in a non-provocative tone. That was a lawless time, and he needed to avoid giving the army any excuse. When we came out of our rooms to see what was going on, we noticed that the soldiers had become less confrontational. There were also some young people in the college whom the provincial had introduced to us as students on "spiritual retreat." It would take us more than twenty years to learn the truth of Father Jorge's rescue efforts.

Scannone believes that the purpose of the raid was intimidatory "as if they were saying, 'we are keeping an eye on you from out here. But we can come into your home any time we want.' However, things would have taken a very different turn that night had they discovered some particular book lying around, a reference to Marx, a 'suspicious' magazine or any other literature considered leftist."

I ask Father Juan Carlos, "In what way did Father Bergoglio defend you from the military junta?" The theologian responds,

> Actually, he also protected me from certain bishops. Those were not easy years. Father Jorge took care of us; it was his duty. As provincial superior of the Jesuits, his first responsibility was the protection of each Jesuit. It is not, therefore, by chance that at the end of those years of massacre no Jesuit had been murdered by the dictatorship—even if now there are some who consider this as a fault. Today, things can be observed and judged with a different perspective, but back then Bergoglio did what anyone in his position had to do. He conferred frequently with Father General [head of the international Jesuit order in Rome], who was aware of what was happening and counseled us on how to avoid trouble and bypass the oppressive control of the regime without abandoning our ideas.

What guidance did Father Bergoglio give Scannone to avoid being "sucked up" in a concentration camp?

His first advice was for me to never mail any of my works or essays through the post office of San Miguel and less still from Buenos Aires. He suspected that all correspondence as well as telephone conversations were being monitored. Therefore, in order for my writings to be published internationally, I needed to utilize post offices far from the capital. In fact, my writings were never subject to censorship by the political police. And my teachings continued to be made known throughout Europe. Also, the provincial advised me to never go out alone into the neighborhoods for pastoral work—and not only for security reasons. I had to make sure someone was always present during all my activities. So if the police, army, navy, or air force came for me, there would always be a witness. These are some of the ways Bergoglio suggested to us so as not to disappear from the face of the earth.

As has been mentioned, Father Bergoglio said nothing to the teachers and students of the college about the true situation of the persecuted people taken in at San Miguel. Father Scannone says, "This was really extraordinary. He never gave any hint. Bergoglio said that the young people who popped in temporarily were there for vocational discernment or that they needed help with their studies. And that's what we believed. We never suspected he was engaged in 'clandestine operations.'"

Scannone only recently discovered that those young people were not there to talk about the priesthood.

> And when these stories finally began emerging, in speaking here with the other Jesuits in the community, we finally realized the real reason he took them in. This means that Father Bergoglio not only kept it secret at that time, but even afterwards he never boasted about his unique mission. I can state the following without a shadow of a doubt, as a direct witness on numerous occasions: Father Bergoglio strove not only to protect, defend and save other Jesuit priests and seminarians, but also to hide young students who were threatened by the dictatorship and were brought to our college out of caution to keep them safe from the police.

Was it possible that the former provincial of the Jesuits maintained secrecy because he did not believe he could not trust anyone? "It was not a matter of a lack of faith in his fellow Jesuits," replies Father Juan Carlos.

> Of course he didn't want us to blow his cover because of our own naivety. Those were years of fear, let's not forget. Father Bergoglio could not risk it. If any one of the Jesuits of the college had been arrested by the military, who could ensure that he would not be tortured into revealing Bergoglio's secret activities? For this reason he

kept it strictly confidential. Additionally, Father Jorge knew that his delicate mission could put not only individual Jesuits in very serious danger but also the entire Company [Jesuit order] in Argentina. If Videla's killers had discovered that the Jesuits of Buenos Aires were conducting illegal activities under the direction of their superior in opposition to the 'National Reorganization Process,' there would have certainly been unimaginable consequences.

Finally, I ask Father Scannone his opinion of the case of Yorio and Jalics:

"Father Jalics has denied any involvement by Bergoglio. Personally, I was sure of that for years. I was a very good friend of Father Orlando Yorio, and sometimes we worked together on theological matters. Since Bergoglio was living in our house in San Miguel at the time the two priests disappeared, he spoke to me about what he was doing. He shared with me about how he was trying to find out who had abducted them and where they were being imprisoned. Even the vicar bishop of the area, Monsignor Mario Serra, informed us about the investigations he [Bergoglio] was making to obtain their release. I can testify to Father Provincial's concern and commitment to set them both free. The military denied having arrested them, but news leaked out that they were being held at the Navy School of Mechanics [ESMA]. When the jailers realized that Jalics and Yorio were innocent, they kept them for months."

Did perhaps the military want to keep the two prisoners hostage to soften the positions of the Jesuits? "Possibly, but in my opinion they kept them imprisoned because they did not know how to get out of the situation [after realizing they were innocent]," says Father Juan Carlos. "Bergoglio was able to gather precise information, and he had the generals cornered. Eventually they were released, but in such a way that they could not give precise details about those who had detained and tortured them. Throughout the period of detention, both were kept hooded, and they were drugged prior to being released. We should also recognize that it was due to the assistance of Father Provincial that both were able to find shelter abroad in order not to end up desaparecidos again."

PART THREE

ANSWERS FOUND

CHAPTER 14

AMNESTY INTERNATIONAL

"No accusation against Bergoglio"

A MNESTY International quickly prepared a document "exclusively for internal use only" the day after the white smoke signaled Jorge Mario Bergoglio had become bishop of Rome on March 13, 2013. The international human rights organization had long studied the Argentine case. There were reports consisting of millions of pages, hundreds of witnesses, and a mountain of evidence against the regime. They had an archive of names and stories that contributed to more research leading to the discovery that some former torturers had returned to hide in the strange ordinariness of a country in which even the truth had long seemed to disappear.

A few hours after the final ballot in the Sistine Chapel, the phone began ringing off the hook in Amnesty offices scattered throughout the world. Journalists and activists were looking for a comment about the new pontiff. In the organization's New York headquarters, a memo was drafted summarizing what line to take with the media. They sifted through their archives, queried their databases multiple times, and searched for a name: *Bergoglio*. Nothing. They then called on those activists who had been the most involved with the plight of the desaparecidos, but not even they could recall any accusation which turned out to be even partially grounded.

With the prudence owed to an affair whose legal outcome had not yet been settled, Amnesty provided management with clear guidance. The document, which I am reproducing here, is key to understanding the "Bergoglio case." At least for how this came to be known and followed by an organization whose independence is not in question.

Following is the original text:

> *AMNESTY INTERNATIONAL*
> *QUESTIONS AND ANSWERS – INTERNAL*
> *INTERNAL DOCUMENT – NOT TO BE USED*
> *FOR MAKING PUBLIC STATEMENTS OR*
> *PRESS RELEASES – ONLY FOR REACTIVE USE*
>
> *14 March 2013*

The Catholic church and new Pope's role during the last Argentine military regime (1976–1983).

On Wednesday 13 March 2013 a new Pope—the highest authority within the Catholic Church—was elected. The person designated for the position is the Argentine Jesuit Jorge Mario Bergoglio, who chose the name of Francisco. Until his election, Cardinal Bergoglio was the Archbishop of Buenos Aires, Argentina.

—What does Amnesty International think of the election of the new Pope, who has been linked to human rights violations during Argentina's military regime?

The tragedy experienced in Argentina between 1976 and 1983, when the military regime was responsible for systematic violations of human rights, has undone the lives of thousands of people. Amnesty International has worked for years looking for truth, justice and reparation for the crimes committed by the previous military government in Argentina and by other military regimes in countries in the region (such as Chile, Uruguay, Paraguay and Bolivia) during the 70s and 80s. During that time, Amnesty International documented and denounced thousands of cases of disappearances, torture, extrajudicial killing and abduction of children, and campaigned for the perpetrators of such acts to be brought to justice.

Amnesty International takes no position on the person who holds the position of Pope, or how he is chosen.

In relation to any possible links of the former archbishop of Buenos Aires to the commission of human rights violations, the organization states that they must be investigated impartially and independently as in the case of any other person.

This statement should not be interpreted in any case in the sense that Amnesty International grants or denies credibility to such possible links.

—What was the role of the Catholic Church in Argentina during the military regime?

Amnesty International is aware of allegations linking the Catholic Church with the authorities of the military regime in Argentina and its possible involvement or participation in human rights violations.

Amnesty International, however, does not believe that it is possible to generalize on the role of the Catholic Church in Argentina or in any other country in the region.

There have been different types of complaints regarding the role played by the Catholic Church during the military regime. They range from the charge of failing to act against human rights violations (e.g., omitting support the search for those missing or not interceding in special cases before the authorities) to delivering opponents into the hands of the regime.

Some members of the Church have been brought to justice in Argentina. The life sentence imposed on Christian Von Wernich, former chaplain of the Buenos Aires police, is public knowledge. Von Wernich was sentenced in October 2007 for his role in 42 hijackings, 7 murders and 31 cases of torture (news.bbc.co.uk/1/hi/world/americas/7035294.stm and www.amnesty.org/es/region/argentina/report-2008).

We should not forget that within the church in Argentina and the region were many who opposed these regimes and suffered intimidation, torture, disappearance or execution. Many of them worked and continue to work for the promotion and protection of human rights for all without discrimination.

—What was the role of the new Pope during the dictatorship? Was he involved in human rights violations?

In the case of Jorge Mario Bergoglio, Amnesty International knows of a case opened in 2005 of the disappearance of two Jesuit priest, but has no documentation to prove or discount the participation of the new Pope in these events. No imputation or formal charge has been made against Jorge Mario Bergoglio and we have no record in our archives of any involvement of the former Archbishop of Buenos Aires in other cases.

A case by case analysis of any possible link of the new Pope with any case of human rights violations during the Argentine military regime is the role of Argentina's justice system. No one can be above the law when it comes to human rights violations. Not even the Pope.

—Has Argentinean justice done anything about human rights crimes committed during the military regime?

Amnesty International has expressed several times its satisfaction with the progress made by the Argentinean justice system regarding the prosecution of perpetrators of human rights violations committed during the military regime in the country and the region. Argentina is the most advanced South American country in this regard.

Emblematic cases have been resolved in recent years: in July 2012, former Argentine presidents Jorge Rafael Videla and Reynaldo Bignone were convicted of the systematic kidnapping of children and sentenced to 50 and 15 years' imprisonment respectively. In October 2011, former navy captain Alfredo Astiz and fifteen other men were sentenced to prison terms ranging from 18 years to life imprisonment for involvement in 86 crimes against humanity committed in a secret detention centre of the College of Naval Mechanics (ESMA, in Spanish initials) in Buenos Aires.

Recently, the trial opened in Argentina against South American leaders responsible for Operation Condor, an international conspiracy of collaboration between Argentina, Bolivia, Brasil, Chile, Paraguay, Peru and Uruguay to arrest, exchange and eventually kill those opposing the regimes in the 70s and 80s.

Reynaldo Bignone, the last president of the Argentine military regime, was sentenced to life imprisonment for the Campos de Mayo's case this week.

Amnesty International will continue supporting the victims of human rights violations and their relatives to reach truth, justice and reparations. The organization trusts that the Argentinean justice will maintain its exemplary role against impunity for crimes during the past.

CHAPTER 15

CONCLUSION

A few hours after his election to the throne of Peter that wet evening on March 13, 2013, half the world's Internet websites were already boiling with accusations, conspiracies, and speculations on the role Jorge Mario Bergoglio played during the dictatorship in Argentina. Old compromising photos and faded documents were re-circulated, suggesting weaknesses in the new pontiff during the dramatic period of the desaparecidos. Symptomatic was the front page of the [Italian communist newspaper] *Manifesto*. The full-page headline brandishing a photo of the new bishop of Rome on March 14 read, "He is not Francis," followed by an explanation: "In his background there are lights of a choice of poverty mixed with the darkness of a past close to the Peronist right-wing."

I started investigating that same night a few hours after Pope Francis appeared on the central loggia of St. Peter's basilica. It didn't take long to determine that the images on the web portraying him with dictator Videla were fake. Even documents that were supposedly the lynchpin of his guilt smelled rotten.

While rummaging around in Bergoglio's past, clues began to gradually emerge leading me to the "list." I was open to every possibility—both positive and negative. Would my research fully rehabilitate the former Superior of the Jesuits of Argentina or would it sentence him to life with no chance of appeal? I was not interested in writing hagiography. On the contrary, as a police reporter, I knew that the discovery of indisputable proof of Bergoglio's collusion with the monsters who ruled Argentina from 1976 to 1983 would have been a sensational hit. I must admit that the discovery of such a story would not have given me joy; on the contrary it would have caused me profound distress, only partly compensated by having written a sensational international scoop. But a serious reconstruction of events does not allow for pre-conceived notions or prejudices.

Instead, I discovered documents and testimony that excluded any complicity with the regime; on the contrary, they clearly demonstrate how he helped those who were persecuted by the junta. This was confirmed beyond a shadow of a doubt by various people and associations: from Nobel Peace Prize winner, Adolfo Pérez Esquivel, to the presiding judge who investigated the crimes committed by the dictatorship, Germán Castelli, all the way to organizations notoriously known for being rigorous and far from "Catholic" sympathies, such as Amnesty International.

As my journalistic investigation progressed, from time to time, I began to hear about dissidents who had been protected and saved by the future pope during those terrible years. As background noise that slowly gets louder and louder, a desire welled up within me to give these voices a name, a face, a story. I began to look for evidence. First there was one, then two, ten, and finally even more. After many decades, these people decided not to grant the torturers of that era yet another victory: deceptions about Bergoglio.

I must admit that it was difficult to get those on the "list" to talk, as I have already mentioned. Initially, I had no explanation for their reticence. Why did everyone I met—and who owed their life to Father Jorge—not want to shout it from the rooftops? Far from being complicit with the butchers dressed in camouflage, they knew that the new bishop of Rome had actually acted in the background risking his own hide and that of his entire religious order to save, hide, protect, and expatriate many who for various reasons were persecuted by the regime rampaging in the *pampas*.

The silence, as I noted in the introduction, was not a desire to minimize or hide something. It is part of the persona of Francis, who—I repeat without desiring to make this a hagiography since the facts speak for themselves—seems to have fully incarnated the dictate of the Gospel of Matthew in chapter six when Jesus speaks of almsgiving: "do not let your left hand know what your right is doing" (cf. Matthew 6:3).

On several occasions, people both in Argentina and in Italy helped me understand that it was actually

the future pope himself who—through hints, sugges-
tions, and subtle words—led them to be silent and humble. He was conscious of the fact that overt promotion
of the good he accomplished in the 1970s for so many
could have been chalked up simply as Vatican market-
ing and propaganda. In short, he believed it better to be
silent about his own merits than to be charged with self-
promotion. I believe this was—if I may permit myself to
think so and say so—the course of action of Father Jorge
Mario who became Francis.

I also must add *pro domo mea*, but it is the truth, that I
never had any Vatican support during this project. There
were no meetings, no words of advice, nothing. My work
was born purely of a *curiositas* that dwells within every
reporter: the desire to understand, explore, and discover
something new, as well as my conviction—which slowly
matured as the "list" grew with stories, voices, words and
faces—that good triumphs in the end and must triumph.
In this case, the goodness of actions of charity and intelligence on the part of Father Jorge: charity to those who
turned to him for decisive help, intelligence for how he
knew how to move in that Argentine morass (even at
home, in the church) during those years.

I hope that this book has achieved a small, but valuable result: now, thanks to the witnesses on the "list," we
know with certainty on whose side Bergoglio was fighting during that messy and dramatic period of his people's
suffering. And while the completion of this book drew to
a close, other stories and witnesses surfaced: former students, seminarians, catechists, and others who escaped

from the clutches of military repression. All were grateful, in the depths of their heart, to a man now called Francis, in whom they found support until a few months before his election as Roman Pontiff. In short, "Bergoglio's list" is not yet concluded.

APPENDIX

QUESTIONING OF CARDINAL BERGOGLIO in the "ESMA TRIAL" OF 2010

*O*N November 8, 2010, the tribunal [tasked with] judging the crimes committed in ESMA entered the residence of the Archbishop of Buenos Aires next to the cathedral in Plaza de Mayo.

Jorge Mario Bergoglio was summoned at 11:30. In accordance with local law, the cardinal was allowed to be questioned at his residence. After three hours and fifty minutes of direct, repetitive, and sometimes suffocating questions, one of the most anticipated interrogations of the trials of the military junta came to a close.

There is no paper or even a notepad to take notes [lying] on the table [in front of him]. Judges Daniel Obligado, Germán Castelli, and Ricardo Farias were seated to his left. In front of them, are an array of hardened attorneys from various human rights associations, some relatives of victims, and others under investigation. The attorneys of Bergoglio attend the hearing as well.

What follows is the published transcript of the questioning. We have deliberately omitted some responses of repetitious content and references to events and people who are unconnected to culpability and who, forty years after the facts, should no longer be continually dragged through events to which they are totally irrelevant.

Luis Zamora, the attorney representing the victims, bombarded the then archbishop with ever more insidious questions without giving Bergoglio a break. This is another reason why the three judges concluded that no culpability was attributable to the cardinal archbishop.

The entire deposition was videotaped. The tapes, which we watched thanks to local legal sources, are kept in the archives of the tribunal. (The footnotes and those in in brackets are from the translator.)

Buenos Aires, November 8, 2010
Bergoglio testifies before the TOF [Oral Federal Tribunal] N. 5.
ID no. 4.202.826
Parents: Mario José Francisco and Regina Sívori

BERGOGLIO: Provincial of the CG [Company of Jesus], until December 8, 1979.

ZAMORA: Were you aware of the abduction of family members and of a religious sister in the church of Santa Cruz in December, 1977?

BERGOGLIO: From the media. It was a group of people who worked for human rights and they met there. There were two French religious sisters and an acquaintance of mine, Esther Ballestrino de Careaga.*

ZAMORA: Do you know if the hierarchy denounced this case?

BERGOGLIO: I cannot be sure, but I assume so, in the manner in which it was customary to denounce these cases, since it dealt with a Catholic Church.

ZAMORA: Would there be evidence in some central archive of the Catholic Church?

BERGOGLIO: I assume so, but I do not know.

ZAMORA: Is that archive under your authority?

BERGOGLIO: The central archive of the CEA [Argentine Episcopal Conference] is under the authority of the CEA.

ZAMORA: And who presides over the CEA?

BERGOGLIO: I do.

ZAMORA: Would there be a way to find it?

BERGOGLIO: I don't know about finding it, but search for it, yes.

---

* Esther Ballestrino de Careaga (1918–1977) was one of the founders of the movement of the Mothers of Plaza de Mayo. On December 8, 1977, she was abducted and brought to ESMA together with two French nuns, Alice Domon and Léonie Duquet, to a command center of the dictatorship. There, she was tortured for ten days and subsequently killed, thrown in one of the infamous "death flights." Her remains were found on the shores of Buenos Aires in 1978 and thrown in a common grave. They were identified only in 2005.

ZAMORA: In what circumstances did you meet E. B. de Careaga?

BERGOGLIO: She was my boss of the laboratory of chemical analysis where I worked in 1953, '54 and a strong friendship developed between the two of us. She was Paraguayan.

ZAMORA: When you learned of her abduction, did you do anything?

BERGOGLIO: It pained me greatly, I tried to get in contact with a family member, but I couldn't. They were in hiding a bit. A daughter of hers had been detained and then released. I tried to speak with people who could do something for her.

ZAMORA: To whom are you referring?

BERGOGLIO: People, close [to her], who could get around, human rights people.

ZAMORA: And the authorities?

BERGOGLIO: No, because that was under the jurisdiction of the Archdiocese of Buenos Aires, and I was provincial of the Jesuits.

ZAMORA: Were you or had you had close contact with Mrs. de Careaga?

BERGOGLIO: A fair amount. I took the actions I was able to take.

ZAMORA: See if you can make an effort to explain to us with greater precision.

BERGOGLIO: I went to people who knew her to get them involved in finding her whereabouts. Some dealt with the ODH [Organizations for human rights], some not, people who had access to the authorities at that moment. I also spoke with several officials at the archbishop's office. With Mons. Olmedo, who dealt with the legal part.

ZAMORA: Afterwards, did you follow up in finding out what action Mons. Olmedo had taken?

BERGOGLIO: Yes, he told me that he had made some contacts, but that he did not have specific information on where she was being held nor anything else.

ZAMORA: In what year and in what circumstances did you meet Orlando Yorio and Francisco Jalics?

BERGOGLIO: I believe I met Yorio in '61, '62, in the Colegio Máximo, which is the Jesuit house of studies, where the School of Philosophy and Theology is. Later he was my professor of theology on the tract, *De Trinitate*. I met Jalics in '61, I believe in the same place. He was professor of fundamental theology, one of the parts, and during my first two years I had him as spiritual advisor.

ZAMORA: [When did you meet] Ricciardelli?*

BERGOGLIO: Yes, I met him in 1992 when he was vicar bishop of Flores.

ZAMORA: Do you remember if a problem emerged regarding the vows of Father Yorio in 1975/76?

---

* Father Rodolfo Ricciardelli was one of the founders of the Movement of Priests for the Third World. He worked in the *villa miseria* slums of Bajo Flores, or 1.11.14, as it will often be referred to in the text. He died in 2008. Others within the Argentine church in those years who will be referenced are Bishops Enrique Angelelli, Adolfo Tórtolo and Vicente Faustino Zazpe; they did not take part in the Movement themselves, but they gave it tacit approval.

BERGOGLIO: I can say that he never broke any of the three, at least publically and as far as I know.

ZAMORA: Within the Company of Jesus, were there any accusations regarding the way in which Fathers Yorio and Jalics carried out their priestly role?

BERGOGLIO: Nothing in particular. In that period, any priest who worked with the poorest margins of society was the target of suspicions and accusations. In June of 1973, I traveled to La Rioja with the previous [Jesuit] provincial to intervene in the case of two Jesuits who were in the missions there and worked with the poor of the region and who were also object of these rumors. It was something very common: anyone who went to work with the poor was [considered] a leftist, and this way of thinking did not end then. Two months ago, a layperson who worked in one of the villas of Buenos Aires received a comment: "So, you returned to work with that leftist." It was something that already existed for many years. But, regarding accusations of an ideological sort, that they belonged to subversive groups—as they were called then—I never received such from reasonable people.

ZAMORA: From what sectors of society did the accusations come from?

BERGOGLIO: People who were not in agreement with that particular pastoral choice.

ZAMORA: Do they not have a first and last name?

BERGOGLIO: No. Sectors, people. In fact, in August of 1974, when Father Arrupe visited La Rioja with me while I was already provincial, many sectors of

Society of La Rioja publically expressed indignation over our visit to Jesuits who were working with the very poor.

ZAMORA: It is important that you make an effort to recall where the accusations came from regarding Yorio and Jalics to which you referred earlier.

BERGOGLIO: From the same environments, from different ideologies, across the board. Certain sectors of society or from cultural people who were not in agreement with that choice, a very well defined choice within the Church.

ZAMORA: It is very important that you make an effort to remember the first and last name of members of the Company of Jesus, of the Catholic Church, of the hierarchy who accused them or who supported this type of accusation.

BERGOGLIO: It was a general criticism against all those who shared this type of pastoral choice.

ZAMORA: But on behalf of whom?

BERGOGLIO: Of diverse sectors, across the board. It was spoken, it was said, it was published in the journals.

ZAMORA: Did they speak to you?

BERGOGLIO: It was spoken about in the communities, in sectors, in some parishes. In all sectors of the Church. And even outside.

ZAMORA: You do not remember one concrete case, some bishop, some cardinal?

BERGOGLIO: No, because it was something very common. Even if you try not to take them seriously, not the accusations, but their significance, even if not true, they are all convinced that priests who work with the poor are leftists.

ZAMORA: That was risky, because such was the same type of accusation the dictatorship used to arrest people. Does this not help you to more concretely specify where these accusations came from?

BERGOGLIO: Fathers Jalics and Yorio left the Company before the military coup, and we can use the death of Father Mugica as an historical reference, which came before the coup.*

ZAMORA: I don't understand. The question was if you could remember who fomented these criticisms, those which you "don't take seriously."

BERGOGLIO: Let me clarify the expression, "don't take seriously." It's not that I did not consider calumny as something grave. Calumny is a grave sin. I do not diminish this. But we already lived in that environment and had to stand by those who made this type of choice. I say it from the point of view of a person who was accustomed to listening to these types of accusations for a long time before the military coup.

[...]

ZAMORA: Regarding the [Superior] General of the Jesuits, do you know if he expressed accusations or if he agreed with them?

---

* Father Carlos Mugica (1930–1974) was an Argentine priest of the Movement of Third World Priests. He did most of his ministry in Villa del Retiro and was shot to death in 1974. For this reason Bergoglio underlines that his murder took place before the coup, which was in 1976.

BERGOGLIO: No, he was a man who supported working with the poor.

ZAMORA: This included Fathers Yorio and Jalics.

BERGOGLIO: Yes.

ZAMORA: When did Father Yorio quit giving lectures?

BERGOGLIO: I don't remember.

ZAMORA: And so you don't know why either?

BERGOGLIO: Courses finished and then began again, they were cyclical.

ZAMORA: Did you have a close relationship with Father Yorio?

BERGOGLIO: A normal relationship between two brother Jesuits. We were not friends, but nor were we enemies. But we had good relations.

ZAMORA: Did he not tell you, however, why he quit teaching?

BERGOGLIO: I don't remember, but what I can say now is that it must have been due to the cyclical nature of the courses.

ZAMORA: Do you remember if you consulted Father Jalics in your role as provincial regarding the accusations that he and Father Yorio were receiving?

BERGOGLIO: Yes, and not only the two of them, but all the Jesuits who had chosen this lifestyle with regards to poverty. It was normal that we talked about things. And to see how to proceed.

ZAMORA: And in the case of Yorio and Jalics?

BERGOGLIO: Yes, as with everyone, it was routine.

ZAMORA: Since we are investigating what happened to them here, it is important that you remember what they said to you, what conversations took place, what your reaction was as provincial, of the hierarchy . . .

BERGOGLIO: The relationship was good.

ZAMORA: No. The reaction.*

BERGOGLIO: To continually take cautious measures. It is necessary, however, also to clarify that this was not the only work they undertook, and that, moreover, they did not live in the villas. They lived in the Rivadavia neighborhood, and they worked doing the [spiritual] exercises, giving spiritual direction, giving classes, and above all Father Jalics was also a writer. And on the weekend, they helped in Villa 1.11.14 [the neighborhood of Bajo Flores].

ZAMORA: Had any ecclesiastical authority made an agreement with the military junta that before a priest was detained the bishop under whose authority he was had to be notified?

BERGOGLIO: No.

ZAMORA: You have never heard this?

BERGOGLIO: No.

ZAMORA: Do you know what happened to Jalics, Yorio and a group of catechists in the Rivadavia neighborhood?

BERGOGLIO: On what date?

ZAMORA: In May of 1976.

BERGOGLIO: Are you referring to their abduction?

ZAMORA: I cannot suggest to you the response.

---

*   Bergoglio confused the term, *reacción*, "reaction," with *relación*, "relation" or "relationship."

BERGOGLIO: Around the 22nd or 23rd of May, there was a raid and they were detained (tapping with his finger, *registrar's note*).

ZAMORA: Do you know who was detained and what the operation consisted of?

BERGOGLIO: I know that Fathers Jalics and Yorio were detained together with a group of laypersons and also that some were released, I heard, in the first few days.

ZAMORA: Do you know if their license had been suspended?

BERGOGLIO: I heard this, but I don't know. The fact that they undertook their pastoral work in the Villa 1.11.14 would indicate that they were able to do so. It would be difficult for a pastor to collaborate with someone whose license had been formally suspended.

ZAMORA: If not formally, in what other way could it have been?

A JUDGE: On whose authority would the suspension of licenses depend?

BERGOGLIO: On the local bishop.

JUDGE: But were the two priests under the authority of the local bishop or of the order?

BERGOGLIO: They were under the authority of the order until they left it. There was a period of transition. And after, when they were incardinated, they were under the authority of the local bishop.

PRESIDING JUDGE: And during the transition?

BERGOGLIO: I told them that they could continue to celebrate Mass until they were incardinated.

PRESIDING JUDGE: Is it possible that the bishop could have negated the authorization?

BERGOGLIO: As a possibility, yes. But I don't know.

ZAMORA: However, in this case they had not found an accommodating bishop.

BERGOGLIO: I am referring to the local bishop, the bishop of Buenos Aires, Cardinal Aramburu.

ZAMORA: Do you know if Aramburu had made a decision regarding them?

BERGOGLIO: Not that I'm aware of.

[…]

ZAMORA: During the transition could they celebrate as any other priest?

BERGOGLIO: I left the interpretation up to them.

ZAMORA: Were they not in the same condition as any other priest?

BERGOGLIO: They were in the period of transition.

ZAMORA: The suspension of one's license, what consequences does this bring?

BERGOGLIO: That he cannot exercise his ministry; the license is jurisdictional.

ZAMORA: Considering that they were in a degree of high exposure and risk in the historical-social period taking place and this situation of not being under the authority of anyone during the transition, could they have had difficulty in celebrating Mass?

BERGOGLIO: Difficulty in celebrating the Mass, no, because I told them they could celebrate. That they were in a degree of high exposure and risk . . .

[…]

PRESIDING JUDGE: Did you accompany them, was there a relationship that continued with Fathers Jalics and Yorio?

BERGOGLIO: Yes, I also offered them the possibility of living in the provincial curia with me, as well as to Dourron. [Luis Dourron was another Jesuit who was abducted in Bajo Flores together with Father Enrique Castellini.] There was already the rumor of the possibility of a raid, at least until they found an accommodating bishop. They thanked me.

[...]

ZAMORA: How did you discover this?

BERGOGLIO: By phone, at noon a person called me from the neighborhood, someone I did not know, saying there had been a raid and that they had arrested two priests and many laypersons, and that Father Dourron was passing by on bicycle and as soon as he saw the raid he escaped down *Varela* street.

ZAMORA: Did you not ask the name of your caller?

BERGOGLIO: No. During a shock like that the last thing that comes to mind is to ask who is calling.

PRESIDING JUDGE: Do you remember what you did upon hearing the news?

BERGOGLIO: Yes, I began to get busy, to speak with some priests I believed had contacts with the police, with the Armed Forces. We got moving immediately.

PRESIDING JUDGE: Did you obtain information different from what the neighbor provided you with?

BERGOGLIO: They confirmed what had happened, but no one knew where they had taken them. Then they began to say that it had been members of the Navy. After two or three days. Or at least that's what they told me.

PRESIDING JUDGE: Did you update the other ecclesiastical hierarchies regarding the event?

BERGOGLIO: All members of the Company of Jesus. And I also went to the archbishop's office. It was a Sunday, I notified Cardinal Aramburu on Monday or Tuesday, and also the nunciature, Mons. Laghi.

ZAMORA: How did you know that it had been the Navy?

BERGOGLIO: That's what was said, *vox populi* [Latin: voice of the people]; those who had looked into it pointed in that direction.

PRESIDING JUDGE: Did this prompt a different strategy?

BERGOGLIO: Yes, in fact I met the commander of the Navy, Massera, twice. The first time he listened to me and said he would look into it. I explained to him that those two priests had nothing to do with anything unusual. He said that he would let me know. Given that he never let me know, after a couple of months, I asked to have a second meeting while continuing other efforts. I was almost sure it was them [the navy] who were holding them. The second meeting was ugly, it did not last even ten minutes. He told me, "Look, what happened is I already told [Archbishop] Tórtolo." I told him, "You told Mons. Tórtolo, really?" "Well, yes." I then told him, "Look, Massera, I want them to appear." Then I got up and left.

ZAMORA: Where did the stories come from, according to which it was the Navy?

BERGOGLIO: I don't know, but it was a *vox populi*. The people who spoke about it said it had been the Navy.

ZAMORA: What people?

BERGOGLIO: Influential people, those who consulted with, who had connections with judges, with the police, with the military, with the Ministry of the Interior, with the government. And all of them pointed to the Navy.

ZAMORA: Do you remember the names of some of these people who had easy access to those in power?

BERGOGLIO: No.

ZAMORA: Were they your ecclesiastical superiors, the cardinal?

BERGOGLIO: All those to whom one could turn to in a moment of desperation—friends or acquaintances.

ZAMORA: The fact that they knew they had been abducted by the Navy is a detail of enormous importance. If you can make an effort to remember who said it, that which you believed so plausible as to repeat to Massera, would make this person a serious source.

BERGOGLIO: It is said that *vox populi*, *vox Dei*: [Latin expression meaning "the voice of the people is the voice of God"]; it was not one person, it was an agreement. I don't remember if they identified or not even the agents who identified themselves as a Navy task force.

ZAMORA: You do not remember who called you on the telephone, you do not remember who told you that it was the Navy. . . .

PRESIDING JUDGE: There were a lot of them.

ZAMORA: This is why I am asking him to identify at least one.

PRESIDING JUDGE: Do you remember what motiviated you to meet Massera?

BERGOGLIO: Because I was sure, excuse me, almost convinced, that it was him. Because everyone said it. I remember a Jesuit priest who did an excellent job in confirming this hypothesis—Father Fernando Storni.

ZAMORA: Is he still alive?

BERGOGLIO: No. He is dead.

ZAMORA: How curious.

BERGOGLIO: Also [I met] Videla twice, for the same reason. (Court transcriptionist's note: He doesn't remember the exact date, but he calculates that the first meeting must have been granted to him two months after they were abducted). He was very formal, he took note of everything; he said he would look into it. I told him that it was rumored that it had been the Navy. The second time, however, I managed to find out who the chaplain was who went there to celebrate Mass at his house, in the residence of the commander in chief. I asked him to call in sick, so that I could replace him. That Saturday, after Mass, I asked to speak with him [Videla]. There, he gave me the impression that he would get more involved and that he would take things more seriously. But it was not violent like the encounter with Massera.

[...]

ZAMORA: Did you leave any written testimony of those conversations?

BERGOGLIO: I always kept Father General [of the Jesuit order in Rome] informed.

ZAMORA: Through written means?

BERGOGLIO: No. To hasten things in that period email, fax did not yet exist, there was only telex, so I telephoned him directly. I called him from a public telephone on *Calle Corrientes* so as not to use the phone in the curia.

ZAMORA: After having informed him by telephone, did you leave anything written?

BERGOGLIO: No. I phoned him and that's all.

ZAMORA: Is it normal for communications of such importance to be done so orally?

BERGOGLIO: Yes and no. There are some issues that proceed according to a slow, quiet process where one can prepare the necessary memoranda. Others, such as this which were urgent and there was a danger to life based on what was said, had to be expedited quickly.

[...]

ZAMORA: Did you communicate with the relatives of Fathers Yorio and Jalics?

BERGOGLIO: Yes, regarding Father Jalics there were two letters. One to his mother who was in the United States, in which I comforted her by telling her everything we were doing, and another to his brother, who was in Munich. I remember perfectly the meeting I had with either the brother or the brother-in-law of Yorio. It seems that there was a second meeting, but I cannot confirm it.

ZAMORA: Did you inform them of the efforts you were taking?

BERGOGLIO: Yes.

ZAMORA: Did you go to the families of the catechists who were victims of that operation?

BERGOGLIO: I met Dr. Mignone, I do not remember if there was a second time.

PRESIDING JUDGE: What role did he play? Why do you remember him?

BERGOGLIO: First, because a daughter of his had disappeared, and secondly because we had crossed paths in the building where he lived on Santa Fe Avenue, where a cousin of mine lived. And another time on Holy Thursday in the sacristy of the cathedral, but we did not speak. He had come to meet Monsignor Tórtolo, who was celebrating Mass that day. We crossed paths only.

ZAMORA: Do you remember the content of that meeting?

BERGOGLIO: We spoke of common worries, about his concerns for his daughter and about ours for the priests, and to see what could be done next.

ZAMORA: When did you learn that the catechists who had been abducted during the same raid were freed?

BERGOGLIO: When people spoke about it at that time.

ZAMORA: Did you not try to contact the families or those freed to know what had happened, since Yorio and Jalics were still abducted?

BERGOGLIO: No. I knew that other Jesuits were doing so and they told me the information. They affirmed that it had been a wing of the Navy.

ZAMORA: Why did you not seek direct contact?

BERGOGLIO: [...] Since I was already in contact with the people who were carrying out the negotiations, it seemed to me that this was the best way to proceed. It was not an exclusion.

ZAMORA: To clarify, you knew that these were people who had been abducted during the same raid in which the two priests very close to you had been abducted, and who until a short time earlier were under your authority.

The Presiding Judge objects.

ZAMORA: As the witness realized that he had committed an oversight . . .

PRESIDING JUDGE: In any case, you must ask a question. Mr. Bergoglio, do you recall how you discovered that Fathers Jalics and Yorio had been released? Did you meet with them? When?

BERGOGLIO: Father Yorio called me directly. I told him to not tell me where he was and to not move from that place, and to send someone to me who could communicate a place for our meeting. At that point it was necessary to take all possible precautions. We met and we talked. The problem was getting a passport, because we had to get them out of the country. The nuntio [Pio Laghi] acted very well and accepted my suggestion that they be accompanied to the police department. The secretary of the nunciature went so that nothing would happen to him inside with diplomatic cover. In the case of Yorio, he contacted me several times to discuss his future. [...] We decided that the best thing would be to send him to Rome to study canon law. I saw him on several occasions in Rome during my travels there. Afterwards, I never met him again. With Jalics everything was fast, he went immediately in the States where his mother lived.

PRESIDING JUDGE: What did they tell you?

BERGOGLIO: They told me everything. How they had been hooded, shackled, and after a certain period had been transferred to another department, which seemed to be a house in the same area or close to ESMA where they were convinced they had been. They were sure it was the same area due to the noise of aircraft taking off and landing. And how they freed them, drugged in a field in Cañuelas.

PRESIDING JUDGE: Did they tell you of the conditions in which they were detained?

BERGOGLIO: Yes, quite precarious, painful and humiliating.

PRESIDING JUDGE: What details do you remember?

BERGOGLIO: That they would not let them go even to the bathroom. I don't remember if they said something about food.

PRESIDING JUDGE: Direct corporal punishment?

BERGOGLIO: They did not tell me anything. From their story, I had the impression that their entire detention had been quite torturous, but I do not remember specific acts of torture.

PRESIDING JUDGE: Punches, electrical shocks?

BERGOGLIO: They didn't mention anything. I'm not saying that there weren't, just that they didn't tell me about them.

PRESIDING JUDGE: Any other things?

BERGOGLIO: Insults. More than insults, they would tell them, "Look where you have ended up. Jesus Christ says blessed are the poor, but the poor in spirit, not those you work with."

ZAMORA: Once you discovered all this, what initiatives did you take?

BERGOGLIO: In what sense?

ZAMORA: Legally, publically, within the Church, information to the hierarchy.

BERGOGLIO: The first step was to protect their physical safety. For this reason, I recommended to them that they not say where they were. The second step and my concern was to get them out of the country. Obviously, the local bishop was informed, in Rome by phone. And to arrange the future in the case of Father Yorio in Rome, and his incardination in the diocese of Quilmes.

PRESIDING JUDGE: Do you remember if a denunciation was made to the legal authorities?

BERGOGLIO: I do not remember, and if it was made, it was decided through ecclesiastical means, with the archbishop, or through the CEA, I don't remember, so that it was joined with the other denunciations and they were all presented together.

PRESIDING JUDGE: Would there be a way to access the archives?

BERGOGLIO: Yes. I will have them checked.

ZAMORA: Did Fathers Jalics and Yorio tell you if they had been held individually or in a place where there were other people?

BERGOGLIO: There were other people, but I think the two of them were in a cell alone, at least from what they told me. They could hear other people's voices, but from what they told me, they were by themselves.

ZAMORA: That is, you mean to say that when they left, they were sure there were other abducted people in that place?

BERGOGLIO: Yes, yes.

ZAMORA: You did not think of making an immediate denunciation on behalf of the lives of those people?

BERGOGLIO: We made them all through the ecclesiastical hierarchy.

ZAMORA: And why not through the judiciary, since it was a crime?

BERGOGLIO: Due to internal procedures, we preferred to make all denunciations together through the ecclesiastical hierarchy.

PRESIDING JUDGE: Who had the responsibility to decide whether or not to make a judicial denunciation? Did you inform the superior of your order?

BERGOGLIO: Yes.

PRESIDING JUDGE: Was it the superior of your order who decided if you should refer it to the justice system?

BERGOGLIO: Yes.

[...]

ZAMORA: What was the reaction, opinion, and attitude of Fathers Yorio and Jalics in response to the decision to dissolve their community in the Rivadia neighborhood?

BERGOGLIO: It was a reaction that the vow of obedience allows, which is to "represent." They represent to their superior the reasons for which the community should not be dissolved. It was studied and a conclusion was reached that, despite the representation, it would be dissolved. Father General had to intervene. It was a long process, nearly a year and a half. Father General said that either it gets dissolved or they should find another avenue. They represented, as the constitutions of the Company dictate, properly.

The Presiding Judge asks him to clarify what "represent" means in non-technical language.

BERGOGLIO: When an order is given to someone and this person does not agree, according to the vow of obedience, he has the right [...] to expose the reasons for which he does not consider it convenient, with motives and through good dialogue.

ZAMORA: You said, however, that there was an alternative, to find "other avenues." What were they?

BERGOGLIO: To leave the Company and exercise their ministry outside of it, under the authority of a bishop.

ZAMORA: One can be outside the authority of a bishop or in another congregation?

BERGOGLIO: They would have to look for a bishop or enter into another congregation.

ZAMORA: What happened when their "representation" was rejected?

BERGOGLIO: Then they asked to leave the Company.

[...]

BERGOGLIO: It was dealt with, it was sent to Rome, and when the response arrived, it said that their resignations had been granted, and Father Jalics had permission to begin the process of the indult of secularization; that is, to pass to the secular clergy [i.e. diocesan priesthood]

ZAMORA: When did it happen?

BERGOGLIO: I remember when Fathers Dourron and Yorio were notified of their resignations; it was on March 19, 1976.

ZAMORA: From then, they had to look for a . . .

BERGOGLIO: . . . a bishop. Yes.

[...]

ZAMORA: Do you remember suggesting the two priests speak with the bishop of Morón, Monsignor Miguel Raspanti, or with others?

BERGOGLIO: I suggested several bishops to them, including some they already had a relationship with, like Novak, Zazpe, Raspanti.

ZAMORA: You claim that a report was not mandatory, but rather a customary procedure. Did you give a report to Raspanti?

BERGOGLIO: He called me by phone and we talked about it in a long conversation in which he asked me about each of them.

ZAMORA: I mean to say that the transfer of the two priests

was important, especially because there was a conflict about the opinion of the two priests who had taken recourse to the "representation." In such a case, is it common practice to make a report in writing or not?

BERGOGLIO: It is not necessary, it is not a customary practice. We must provide one if requested in one way or another. In this case it was made verbally, and I cannot remember if I left anything written.

ZAMORA: In the event that there were something written, would there be a way to look for a copy of that report?

BERGOGLIO: Yes, one can always try. There is the possibility.

ZAMORA: Do you know what happened to the efforts of Yorio and Jalics, to whom and what was the outcome?

BERGOGLIO: I know that Monsignor Raspanti accepted one of the three. I suppose that regardless of what was said of one or the other, he was unwilling to accept a group, only one. This is an interpretation of mine that I arrived at through telephone conversations with him.

ZAMORA: Do you remember if Bishop Raspanti went to see them at the Colegio Máximo as part of this exchange?

BERGOGLIO: When Fathers Jalics and Yorio left the Company, the provincial's residence was in Buenos Aires, not in the Colegio Máximo [in San Miguel].

ZAMORA: Was the telephone conversation with Monsignor Raspanti after they left the Company?

BERGOGLIO: When they went to him, he called me to ask my opinion.

[...]

ZAMORA: Did other bishops contact you like Raspanti did?

BERGOGLIO: No.

ZAMORA: Do you know the theologian, Marina Ruby [one of Bergoglio's accusers]?

BERGOGLIO: She was a student in the School of Theology, I think in morality, or maybe she was doing a postgraduate licensure in morality in the School of Theology. It must have been in the '80s.

ZAMORA: To help your memory, do you know or do you remember if Marina Ruby met with Monsignor Raspanti in the Colegio Máximo who was waiting for you to discuss Jalics and Yorio?

BERGOGLIO: I didn't know this.

ZAMORA: Mr. Bergoglio, what was the internal procedure you followed to convey what you had learned by mouth regarding Yorio and Jalics?

BERGOGLIO: Orally, to Mr. Archbishop. Given that I had to travel to Rome, I informed Father General in detail, the Society of Jesus, and the Argentine provinces in separate meetings that we were holding on them.

ZAMORA: Do you know if they made a decision not to make public what they knew or what they suffered?

BERGOGLIO: I don't know.

ZAMORA: Do you know what the hierarchy did after you informed them?

BERGOGLIO: No.

ZAMORA: Did you include the existence of a clandestine

concentration camp in ESMA and the treatment to
which they were subjected?

BERGOGLIO: Yes.

ZAMORA: Did you seek then a response?

*The defense objects saying neither Bergoglio nor the
Catholic Church is on trial.*

*The Presiding Judge allows the question but requests that
Zamora not allege and that he formulate a question.*

ZAMORA: Given that you had informed them, was it customary for them to tell you what had been done, or
did you seek to ask?

BERGOGLIO: They did not inform me.

PRESIDING JUDGE: They did not inform you. And did you
look into knowing if there had been a response?

BERGOGLIO: Yes. Something, in general. I sought
responses, but vaguely. I do not remember the details.

PRESIDING JUDGE: With respect to a judicial denunciation
mentioned earlier, was it made or not?

BERGOGLIO: I am not aware, but I presume so.

PRESIDING JUDGE: What did you do?

BERGOGLIO: I presume so, but I am not sure.

PRESIDING JUDGE: Did it depend on the Superior General
of the order?

BERGOGLIO: On the Superior General of the order and
his approval for it to be done here. It had to be done
here.

PRESIDING JUDGE: And to know something one should
ask the current Superior General of the order, to see
if there is some record?

BERGOGLIO: Either here with the bishops' conference or

with the archbishop, who are the ones who had to take care of these procedures.

ZAMORA: Did the Superior General of the order not live in Argentina?

BERGOGLIO: No.

ZAMORA: And he was the only person authorized to deal with this type of procedure or denunciation, someone who did not live in Argentina, or was there someone else besides you [Bergoglio]?

BERGOGLIO: He usually gave the approval to execute the procedures and where to make them.

ZAMORA: Did the fact that Jalics and Yorio told you what they suffered, and taking into account the fact that you considered the work of Yorio and Jalics, as all those who undertook similar projects, to be the subject of criticism and accusations, push you to do something to protect others?

BERGOGLIO: Yes, to recommend specific security measures. Including the smallest things, sometimes. Specific security measures.

ZAMORA: Do you know if someone said something to you about Yorio or Jalics, or did you learn it through other avenues? That a certain priest went to ESMA to give communion to Jalics and Yorio?

BERGOGLIO: I heard this. But I am not aware of its truth. But I heard so.

ZAMORA: Do you remember from whom you heard it?

BERGOGLIO: Probably from some Jesuits who were checking into it. I don't remember if it was from Father Storni or others.

ZAMORA: Regarding the people who were checking into it and to whom you are referring—and this is very important because they discovered as in the case of Storni where they were or presumed to know where they were imprisoned—were these people close to you?

BERGOGLIO: Some were Jesuits, others laypersons, friends of the Jesuits, they were people who offered [to help]. The important thing here is that it was necessary to keep them from disappearing completely.

ZAMORA: I am referring to the fact that, in order to help us further the investigation, if these people were close to you, could you not identify any of them, apart from Storni?

PRESIDING JUDGE: He already responded, he already said it.

ZAMORA: No, no. Now he is speaking of another situation.

PRESIDING JUDGE: Which one? The following one?

ZAMORA: Certainly. The question was referring to the priest who brought communion.

BERGOGLIO: Yes, it was said, the entire world, Storni would have been one of them, but . . . People said they brought them communion. This was said. Even among the Jesuits.

ZAMORA: You were not just a Jesuit, you were the provincial. Inasmuch as you were provincial, and in hearing this, could you not have arranged for someone to bring them communion in ESMA? A priest, obviously. Did this motivate you or not to do something more than what you were doing?

BERGOGLIO: I don't understand.

ZAMORA: Through all the people around you, laypersons or members of the Company of Jesus, or in the Church, I do not know how much influence you had, but you discover that there was a priest who, according to your version, took communion to the two imprisoned priests and who until a few days before their abduction was under your authority as provincial. Knowing all these things did not lead you to want to do something more, to discover where the priests were, where they were located, where to free them?

BERGOGLIO: The person who brings communion doesn't necessarily have to be a priest. It can also be a layperson. This is more common than one thinks.

[...]

ZAMORA: We are speaking about how you discovered where they were, and how you continued doing the same thing.

BERGOGLIO: I had no certainty that they were in the ESMA detention center, no certainty, until they told me after their release.

[...]

ZAMORA: In retrospect, after everything that happened, including the abduction and the release of the priests and some catechists, did you do something for Francisco Jalics's passport application through the authority of the military dictatorship?

BERGOGLIO: Yes.

ZAMORA: When was it?

BERGOGLIO: I don't remember the date, but I think in '78,

it's possible. I don't remember the exact date.

ZAMORA: What did your intervention consist of?

BERGOGLIO: The priest had to renew his passport. He was Hungarian, either a citizen or resident of Argentina, I'm not sure, but he had an Argentine passport. In those days he was a Hungarian refugee, expatriate, in a stateless situation. The only document with which he could travel about, due to the dictatorship in Hungary, was his Argentine passport, which was about to expire. Shortly before the expiration, he had to come here [to Buenos Aires] to renew it. But in our judgement, it was dangerous. That is why I asked the authorities, upon Father Jalics' suggestion, he himself wrote to me asking me that very thing—that they renew it, that they instruct the embassy in Bonn to renew his passport. The excuse I used was that the trip was very expensive.

ZAMORA: Do you know how the situation ended?

BERGOGLIO: They denied it.

ZAMORA: Do you know the reasons?

BERGOGLIO: No.

ZAMORA: Did you ask why, given that you presented the request?

BERGOGLIO: Yes, they said no, that it was necessary to renew it here.

ZAMORA: And who told you this? What official did you refer to regarding the request?

BERGOGLIO: The person who attended to me at the chancellery. I do not remember who it was, but I know that I presented everything, I explained the situation, and later on they told me that it was not customary, or that they couldn't, or something like that.

ZAMORA: Was or was not Orcoyen the director of religion within the chancellery?

BERGOGLIO: I don't remember.

ZAMORA: But was he the director of religion within the chancellery?

BERGOGLIO: It was the official who attended to me. I know that I was at the chancellery, probably in the passport or Foreign Affairs office, but I do not remember.

ZAMORA: So you did not find out from the official? Did you later learn by some other means why? [he had been denied the renewal]

BERGOGLIO: It was obvious why. They wanted him here.

PRESIDING JUDGE: And is this what they told you or is it a conclusion of yours?

BERGOGLIO: It is my own presumption.

ZAMORA: In the exchange with this official who attended to you, was there only one interview or were there others?

BERGOGLIO: There was just one. I handed him the application, he asked me what had happened to the priest, I explained to him that he had been detained, that they had accused both of being guerrillas, but that they had nothing to do with it, and that's it.

ZAMORA: Do you remember anything else you told him? Apart from the fact that he had been detained, did you tell him by whom, why?

BERGOGLIO: I do not know if I told him that he had been in the *Escuela de mecánica* [ESMA]. I probably told him, I don't remember. If so, I don't think that he would have asked where he had been detained because they knew already; I don't think he asked me that. Yes, I remember—what I always said: that they were detained, accused of being guerrillas, but they had nothing to do with it.

ZAMORA: Why do you use the qualifier of "detainment," [Sp: *detención*] when you knew that Yorio and Jalics were abducted [Sp: *secuestrados*]?

BERGOGLIO: I don't know. It's the vocabulary I used...

[...]

ZAMORA: Have you ever heard of the island, El Silencio, in the Tigre?*

BERGOGLIO: No.

ZAMORA: You've never heard of it, or in that moment you hadn't heard of it?

BERGOGLIO: I do not remember if I have ever heard of it.

ZAMORA: Or of some island that the Catholic Church had in the Tigre?

BERGOGLIO: Right now, I am almost sure that there is only a parish chapel in the Tigre, but not an island.

ZAMORA: Right now, and in the time of the dictatorship?

BERGOGLIO: I don't know.

ZAMORA: When is the last time you saw Jalics and Yorio?

BERGOGLIO: I saw Jalics in Buenos Aires. He comes here often. He asked me permission to teach courses, as priests usually do when they come from the outside,

---

* Tigre indicates both the city as well as the same department in the province of Buenos Aires. The city is on the delta on the Paraná River.

and I granted it to him with much pleasure. Once he came to chat with me, he called me. Another time I remember we concelebrated [Mass] in the cathedral after a course of catechesis. The last time I saw him was about two and half years ago, more or less, here in Buenos Aires.

ZAMORA: And Yorio?

BERGOGLIO: The last time I saw him was in Rome while he was studying. I saw him a few times, maybe three. Later, he returned and was incardinated. I know that later he moved and went to live in Uruguay.

ZAMORA: Do the cardinals have some dossier with your background, your history? Is such a dossier prepared? Does something like this exist, perhaps this is not the correct term?

BERGOGLIO: I don't know, it depends on the Holy See.

ZAMORA: You don't know if the Holy See prepares them?

BERGOGLIO: I don't know.

ZAMORA: I'm referring, for example, to when the college [of cardinals] meets for the election of the new pope.

PRESIDING JUDGE: Don't respond, Mr. Bergoglio, but finish, Dr. Zamora.

ZAMORA: If in this case a dossier accompanies each cardinal with their background and their history?

DEFENSE ATTORNEY (VALLE): Here we are judging neither the Catholic Church, nor Cardinal Bergoglio, nor if this topic had any influence on the election of the pope who succeeded John Paul II. It has nothing to do with the fact of the cause.

PRESIDING JUDGE: I certainly don't see where you're going, however, you can reformulate it.

ZAMORA: In the case in which it existed, to ask him a question regarding certain elements...

PRESIDING JUDGE: Why don't you ask him the question directly?

ZAMORA: In the case of the existence of a dossier, would yours include any reference to the Jalics and Yorio case?

BERGOGLIO: First of all, I don't know if such a dossier exists. Second of all, in the conclave in which I participated they did not give me such a dossier on any cardinal.

ZAMORA: When Jalics and Yorio reported to you what they had been through, did they say anything to you more precisely of torture, of degrading treatment? Could they identify anyone?

BERGOGLIO: No, they could not identify anyone.

PRESIDING JUDGE: And what branch could their captors have belonged to?

BERGOGLIO: They were convinced they were in the *Escuela de mecánica de la Armada*, both in the first period of their detention, or in the second that was in a nearby place.

PRESIDING JUDGE: In a place separate from the rest?

BERGOGLIO: Separate and much smaller. Like a large house, something like that.

ZAMORA: Do you remember what details they told you, why they were convinced of it?

BERGOGLIO: No, but they had no doubts.

ZAMORA: There are no more questions.

Questioning by the prosecutor, Dr. Monaschi

MONASCHI: Do you recall if you ever knew if the funerals of Yorio and Jalics were celebrated while they were still imprisoned?

BERGOGLIO: No, I don't remember.

MONASCHI: Could you briefly tell us what Fathers Jalics and Yorio were like, how you remember them before their abduction?

PRESIDING JUDGE: Are you asking about their personality?

MONASCHI: Yes, how he remembers them.

BERGOGLIO: They were good priests, both very intelligent, good teachers. Jalics had a special gift for spiritual direction. I had him as my spiritual advisor for two years in theology, and Yorio had an excellent perceptiveness mixed with an above average intelligence. This gave rise to a combination that made his theology classes fruitful.

MONASCHI: You also spoke of having had a friendly relationship with Mrs. Esther de Careaga. The same question: what do you remember about her during the period in which you worked together?

BERGOGLIO: A woman who taught me how to work. How to make accurate analyses, in the part of glycerin and these things [...]. She taught me how to work well scientifically. A woman with good humor, a woman who introduced me to knowledge of politics. She was a Febrerist, of the Paraguayan Febrerista Party, exiled here.* She had me read various things, articles written by Barletta, for example. We talked about them, we commented about them. I owe a lot to this woman. Later, me being a priest and all, we kept in contact. Once, she called me and said, "Hey, can you come to my house, because my mother-in-law is not well and I want you to give her the last rites." It seemed strange to me because they were not believers, even though her mother-in-law was, she was somewhat pious, but it seemed strange to me. And she asked me where we could hide her library, because she was under surveillance. They had already abducted a daughter of hers whom they later freed. She had three daughters. I remember her as a great woman and, as much her as Mrs. de Blanco or de Bianco [he does not remember the name well], and at that time Azucena Villaflor who was *trasladada* ["transferred," meaning executed], and I gave permission for them to be buried in the church of Santa Cruz.†

MONASCHI: I have no further questions.

---

* The Febrerist Revolutionary Party of Paraguay was a socialist party founded with the revolution of February 17, 1936. It was officially established as a political party in 1951 by some of its members exiled in Buenos Aires.

† Azucena Villaflor, Esther Ballestrino de Careaga and Maria Ponce were mothers in the Madres de Plaza de Mayo movement, victims of the Argentine dictatorship. In 1977, they were abducted and tortured in ESMA, and later killed.

Questioning by Dr. Rito (civil part)

RITO: In your statements, you mentioned to us that you knew Adolfo Servando Tórtolo. How did you meet him, where, and what role did he have?

BERGOGLIO: He was the archbishop of Paraná, vicar of the Armed Forces and president of the Episcopal Conference. I met him due to his being president of the Episcopal Conference. As provincial of the Jesuits, I would report to him when this issue or other things concerned us. On one occasion they had to remove an assessor of an organization of the Church, and he sent me a letter to let me know what was happening. I went to him to protest the removal. This occurred before or at the same time as this problem of the dictatorship.

RITO: Do you remember the role he had in 1976?

BERGOGLIO: He was the president of the episcopate, archbishop of Paraná and vicar of the Armed Forces.

RITO: Did you ever know whether or not the vicar of the Armed Forces had met with the dictatorship hierarchy?

BERGOGLIO: I never knew anything like "it was held on such and such day," but it is obvious that they met. They surely would have had such a meeting.

RITO: Do you know what it was about?

BERGOGLIO: Surely it would have dealt with this problem of abductions, desaparecidos, but I do not know, these are all my assumptions.

RITO: Did he have any communication with you, did he tell you anything?

BERGOGLIO: No, no. In this case, if you will allow me, I would like to clarify my role on the "board." I was provincial of the Jesuits, appointed at the age of 36, and at that time I was 40, I was very far from the entire episcopal body, from episcopal assemblies. The bishop was not close to me. Only the local bishop to whom one went. If I had been bishop at that time, I would have had a different type of relationship with him and, therefore, would have had more access to information. I say all this to situate my position at that time.

RITO: Can you recall having heard the expression, "slum priests" [Sp: *curas villeros*]?

BERGOGLIO: Yes.

RITO: What does it mean? In what context was it used?

BERGOGLIO: They were priests who worked in the villas. A book just came out on the slum priests. Its author is Silvina Premat. In it, she explains some of the mystique from [Carlos] Mujica until today. But this [term] came earlier. It already existed at the time of the military coup of Onganía.* The most influential person who is still alive is Father Botán.†

RITO: In your opinion, does this have something to do with or does it follow some teaching from the Second Vatican Council?

---

* Juan Carlos Onganía Carballo (1914-1995) took power in a coup in 1966 and governed Argentina until 1970.

† Héctor Botán, Miguel Ramondetti and Rodolfo Ricciardelli were founders of the Movement of Third World Priests.

BERGOGLIO: Yes, even if the option for the poor is from the early centuries of Christianity. It's the same gospel. If today I read in a homily the sermons of the early fathers of the church, [second to third] century, about how the poor should be treated, people would say that my homily sounded Maoist or Trotskyist. The Church has always had as an honor in treating the preferential option of the poor. It considered the poor to be treasures of the Church. When during the persecution of Deacon Lawrence, who was administrator of the diocese, he was asked to bring out all the treasures of the Church [...] he showed up with a host of poor people and said, "These are the treasures of the Church." And I'm talking in the second, third century. The option for the poor comes from the gospel. In the Second Vatican Council, the definition of Church as people of God is reformulated, and from there it is born with much more strength and in Latin America it acquires a strong identity in the second General Conference of Latin American Bishops held in Medellín [Colombia].

RITO: What is your opinion towards the work carried out by the slum priests at the time?

BERGOGLIO: It was varied in the countries of Latin America. In some countries, they were involved in political mediation. For example, reading the Gospel with Marxist hermeneutics. That gave rise to liberation theology. In other countries, they were more closely associated with popular piety and they distanced themselves from political engagement; these chose politics with a capital P, for their promotion of and assistance to the poor. The Holy See expressed two statements at that time regarding liberation theology and explained the differences well. They were very open encouraging work with the poor, but within a Christian hermeneutics, not borrowed from some political worldview.

RITO: I was asking for your opinion with respect to the slum priests who were engaged here in Argentina.

BERGOGLIO: Even in Argentina it is also varied, it depends on the dioceses. I had some very involved in particular political hermeneutics, and others who founded the line followed today, like Father Ricciardelli, Father Botán, who have an excellent stance. The book that just came out puts them on this stance. Of human promotion, of evangelization and care of the people of God. Of the accompaniment of the people of God. It was heroic to live so committed to the poor.

[...]

RITO: A few moments ago, you referred to a meeting you had with Fermín Mignone...

BERGOGLIO: Fermín?

RITO: Dr. Mignone.

BERGOGLIO: Dr. Mignone, yes.

RITO: How many meetings did you have with Mignone?

BERGOGLIO: One, surely. One for sure.

BERGOGLIO'S ATTORNEY: Mr. Bergoglio do not respond. Mr. President, he said he had a meeting, that he doesn't remember a second one, and that he came across him here in the cathedral.

PRESIDING JUDGE: The objection of the defense is pertinent.

RITO: One last question. A little while ago, when you recounted how you applied for the passport on behalf of Father Jalics at the chancellery, you could not remember the name of the officer. My colleague asked you a question regarding Anselmo Orcoyen, do you remember?

BERGOGLIO: The name sounds familiar to me, it sounds familiar. It's been thirty-four years, right? This name sounds familiar, but...

RITO: At some point, did the chancellery ask you for a report prior to issuing its opinion?

BERGOGLIO: No.

RITO: You never created any report at all?

BERGOGLIO: Not at all. Simply the letter handed in there in an office. I think, I think that it was the immigration section or the passport office, something like that, I believe that's what it was, but I don't remember.

RITO: In other words, that was the letter that opened the process.

BERGOGLIO: Yes.

RITO: Thank you. I have no further questions.

[...]

PRESIDENTE: Dr. Bregman [attorney for human rights associations], please.

BREGMAN: How did you discover the existence of clandestine detention centers in Argentina?

BERGOGLIO: The certainty that they existed developed during the first months of the dictatorship. It was then that I realized that there were people "sucked up," as was said at that time.

BREGMAN: When you realized that the priests, Jalics and Yorio, had suffered that misfortune, what were your impressions in that moment? Returning to that time, was it something new? Was it something you had already heard of?

BERGOGLIO: My first feeling was that they would have immediately freed them because they had nothing to accuse them of. I knew there was nothing. The first feeling. Mixed with worry. Also, I was convinced, and still am today fairly convinced that it was not an operation in search of only the two of them, but was instead a round-up that they fell into. I am not sure of this, it is a conviction of mine. So, at first I thought they would get out right away, though we got to work quickly, but I didn't think it would last so long.

BREGMAN: Do you remember how long it lasted, how long they remained desaparecidos?

BERGOGLIO: I believe it was from May through October, right? They got out around Mother's Day.*

BREGMAN: At one point you stated that in one of your meetings with Massera, you told him that "they had nothing to do with anything unusual" or a similar expression. What were you referring to with the phrase "nothing to do with anything unusual"? What would it have been otherwise?

BERGOGLIO: Things of guerrillas, subversives, etc.

---

* Mother's Day is held on the third Sunday of October in Argentina.

BREGMAN: That would be the opposite? That would be interpreted the contrary of "nothing to do with anything unusual"?

BERGOGLIO: It's saying, as if they were involved in subversive acts. The same thing had happened in Mendoza to another Jesuit, Juan Luis Moyano, who... but this was before the dictatorship . . . well, there, we immediately identified where he was being detained. We managed to organize his option of leaving the country and he went to Germany to finish his studies. He had nothing to do with it, but had fallen victim to a raid of catechists.

BREGMAN: Are you aware that Mr. Jalics and Yorio testified during the *Juicio a las Juntas* [trial against the juntas]?

BERGOGLIO: Yes.

BREGMAN: Were you present during their deposition? Did you assist them in any way?

BERGOGLIO: No, no.

BREGMAN: Did you communicate with them before or after their deposition?

BERGOGLIO: At that moment, no. Before, yes.

BREGMAN: But I mean during their deposition, or the day before, I'm asking what you normally do.

BERGOGLIO: No, not the day before.

BREGMAN: You further stated that you saw them on a date, if I understood correctly, very close to their liberation.

BERGOGLIO: Yes.

BREGMAN: How did they seem to you physically? What do you remember?

BERGOGLIO: They seemed intact. Despite all they had been through, they seemed intact. And I suppose that the last period of their captivity they knew that they would be released, so I think that, somehow, it made it less heavy [...]

PRESIDING JUDGE: And physically? Since you knew them before. Overweight, thin?

BERGOGLIO: They had always been thin. Yes, they had lost a little weight. But they did not appear emaciated. This is another reason I suppose they had treated them differently during the final period before their liberation. But this is a hypothesis of mine.

BREGMAN: Did you later read what Jalics and Yorio stated during the Juicio a las Juntas?

BERGOGLIO: No.

BREGMAN: You were never interested in knowing what they stated there?

BERGOGLIO: I was interested in knowing what they did. It seemed good to me. But I did not read it.

[...]

BREGMAN: When did you realize that there were children who were being appropriated by the dictatorship?

BERGOGLIO: That... recently... Well, recently in the sense of maybe ten years ago.

[...]

BERGOGLIO: Perhaps during the Juicio a las Juntas. Around then.

BREGMAN: A little earlier, then.

BERGOGLIO: A little earlier. Around then, more or less, I began to realize it.

BREGMAN: We have spoken several times about documentation which may or may not be provided to the trial.
   In conclusion, I would like to be reminded how this
   court can make use of this valuable documentation,
   since it is public knowledge that the Church has a large
   part of the documentation. This is clear from various
   testimonies, including testimony received during this
   very trial. Before this hearing ends, may it be agreed
   upon and determined how and as soon as possible this
   court may have access to this valuable documentation
   in the archives.

PRESIDING JUDGE: Request it, Doctor.

BREGMAN: I am asking if we can come to an agreement
   in which we can search for and see that documentation.

PRESIDING JUDGE: So the question would be whether the
   witness undertakes to check the archives.

BERGOGLIO: Yes, I have no problem. I will instruct the
   record keepers of the archives do so. In fact, regarding other trials concerning the same topic, we have
   received requests for documentation and we sent
   what we had, everything we had.

BREGMAN: In what trial, do you remember?

BERGOGLIO: No. But I do know that the bishops' conference one year ago, if not more, there was a case in
   which they asked me authorization and I said yes,
   do it.

BREGMAN: These authorizations, when they ask for
   information, do they always come to your office, do
   you always have to see to them?

BERGOGLIO: If it's in the archdiocese yes. I am the one who must give the order to the record keepers of the archive of the archdiocese. If it's in the bishops' conference, right now, yes, because I am the president. When the president changes, it will the new president with consent of the executive commission. But they always say yes, of course.

BREGMAN: I have no further questions.

Doctor Zamora resumes questioning

[...]

ZAMORA: In these thirty-four years since they abducted the two priests close to you, and having learned important details through them including what happened in ESMA, why did you never make a denunciation?

The Presiding Judge does not allow the question.

BERGOGLIO'S ATTORNEY: Because the courts never summoned him.

Judge GERMÁN CASTELLI: What position did Jalics and Yorio have regarding liberation theology?

BERGOGLIO: They had a balanced position. Orthodox and in line with the two directives from the Holy See.

CASTELLI: How was this doctrine seen by the dictatorship?

BERGOGLIO: There were some Latin American people that they took, the people of the dictatorship, as strongholds of the devil, for example, Camilo Torres, the Colombian priest. The dictatorship had a tendency to consider these people as purely revolutionary, Marxist, leftist, as an abandonment of the gospel to the left. As I stated before, yes, there were some who promoted theology with Marxist hermeneutics, something the Holy See did not accept, and others who no, instead sought a pastoral presence among the poor, with the hermeneutics of the gospel. The leaders of the dictatorship demonized all liberation theology, including priests who followed the Marxist hermeneutics—who were few in Argentina when compared to other countries—as well as priests who simply lived their priestly vocation among the poor. They were all in the same bag.

CASTELLI: You referred to the case of Mugica and the French nuns. Have you ever known someone who went desaparecido because the dictatorship accused them of sharing these ideas, putting everyone in the same bag?

BERGOGLIO: The La Rioja case is symptomatic. It began before the dictatorship, on that 13th of June '73 with the throwing of rocks by the shore. I believe it was Yoma territory, that one, and they threw stones at the priests and Angelelli because they worked with the people, and it ended with the death of Angelelli, it ended, let's say in quotation marks, because later the environment continued in a different way, with the shooting death of Father Murias, of Father Longueville, who was French, and of the catechist Pedernera, who was also shot to death. And this was August 4, 1976, the death of Angelelli, and that of Longeville, Murias and Pedernera must have been twenty days or a month earlier. And later there was the case of the Pallotine Fathers. I know that case well because I was Alfredo Kelly's confessor, a man of God who lived the gospel fully. It seemed like a vendetta, unjust tyranny.*

CASTELLI: Did the slum priests run risks due to their pastoral choices?

BERGOGLIO: It was a risky situation and they were aware of it. For this reason they lived very close to each other and supported one another. In other dioceses there were other priests who chose the option of the poor and they disappeared. They were aware that they did not have the same safety as a normal priest in a parish and that it was riskier for the type of apostolate they were doing.

CASTELLI: Did Jalics and Yorio adhere to liberation theology?

BERGOGLIO: They adhered to it, but they were balanced and orthodox in line with the two directives from the Holy See; that is to say that they were within what the Church thinks, without a Marxist hermeneutics.

CASTELLI: Did it have an influence on your decision, the fact that they worked in the villas?

BERGOGLIO: Not at all, because we encouraged work with the poor. During my provincialate they began to push inland, in the poorest places, to the indigenous reserves of Santa Victoria, in the north of Tartagal to missionary outposts with Jesuits who were completely

---

* Five Pallotine fathers, including Alfredo Kelly, were killed in execution style due to a military order in their residence in Buenos Aires in 1976. They were suspected of having links with subversive groups.

dedicated to their mission. They sent me a case. . . .
In La Rioja a priest of Guandacol, a Jesuit, was being
heavily persecuted precisely because of his choice.
These missions were always with an evangelization in
line with the Second Vatican Council and Medellín.

[...]

CASTELLI: What was the position of the Argentine
Church and the Vatican regarding the dictatorship?

BERGOGLIO'S LAWYERS OBJECT

VALLE: They have tried to prosecute the dome [i.e. hier-
archy] of the Catholic Church during the military
dictatorship and prosecute including the cardinal,
they have suggested the possibility that [Bergoglio]
was not the successor of John Paul II due to a dossier
that was circulated [among the cardinals]. If those
questions are allowed, then, symmetrically, you must
give the opportunity to the witness, in some way, to
clarify his position which is under scrutiny here.

[...]

CASTELLI: Could you have made it publically known,
through any means of communication, what happened to Yorio and Jalics?

BERGOGLIO: I have spoken a lot with all people who asked
me, I have made public everything I knew about the
injustice they suffered; my position on this is clear.
I do not give media interviews as a personal choice.
However, I once let a journalist know what happened
so he would know my point of view. Those who know
me know that I have always spoken about all this in
the same tone I have spoken about it this afternoon.

TIMELINE

December 17, 1936: Jorge Mario Bergoglio is born in Buenos Aires to parents who emigrated from the Piedmont [region of northern Italy]. His father, Mario, worked as a railway worker, his mother Regina Sivori, raised five children.

March 11, 1958: Jorge enters in the novitiate of the Jesuit order.

December 13, 1969: Bergoglio is ordained a priest.

April 22, 1972: He makes solemn vows within the Jesuit order.

July 31, 1973: He is elected provincial superior of the Jesuits in the province of Argentina.

March 24, 1976: A military junta headed by General Jorge Videla deposes the government of Isabel Perón in a coup. Videla imposes a neoliberal economy and launches clandestine and repressive military operations on a massive scale.

1977: The "dirty war" is intensified against people suspected of opposing the state. Opponents are persecuted as "subversives." Repressive actions include abduction, torture, and murder. Prisoners are often bound hand and foot and thrown alive into the Río de la Plata. The first protests from family members of desaparecidos begin; the most active are the Mothers of Plaza de Mayo.

1978: The regime hosts the FIFA World Cup in Argentina flaunting "peace" reigning in the country.

1980–1981: General Eduardo Viola succeeds Videla and contends with the head of the Navy, Admiral Eduardo Massera, for political leadership and possible transition toward a formally democratic regime.

1982: Two days after a violent union protest, the third head of the junta, General Leopoldo Galtieri, seeks to launch a spectacular [military] operation with the hopes of winning back popular support. On April 2, he orders the military occupation of the Falkland Islands, the British archipelago sought by Argentina. The United Kingdom responds and quickly defeats Argentina leading to the downfall of the regime. During the month of June, General Reynaldo Bignone assumes the presidency.

1983: Bignone calls for democratic elections on October 30. The radical Raúl Alfonsín is victorious and assumes power on December 10. He announces indictments against the former commanders of the military juntas.

1984: Trials against the military accused of human rights violations begin first in the military courts and later in civilian courts. Due to initiative of the government, a special commission (CONADEP), headed by writer Ernesto Sábato, ascertains that 8,900 people were desaparecidos. According to later research carried out by human rights organizations, the number missing would rise to 30,000.

1985: Videla and four other former commanders are sentenced to long prison sentences (two of them to life imprisonment).

1986: Trials against other soldiers cause unrest among the military.

1987: During Holy Week a revolt takes place within the military who support soldiers refusing to testify in the trials. A few weeks later at the request of President Alfonsín, Congress approves a new law of "dutiful obedience." This exempts soldiers from being tried for crimes committed during the regime.

1988: The ultranationalist *carapintadas* organize two military uprisings demanding that further trials be suspended and that the "struggle against subversives" be recognized. They maintain that there had not been a repressive dictatorship, but a harsh and necessary war between subversives and the military called in to restore order.

1990: President Carlos Menem, who succeeded Alfonsin in 1989, grants pardon to five convicted former commanders.

May 20, 1992: After holding various positions in academia and pastoral fields, Bergoglio is appointed auxiliary bishop of Buenos Aires.

June 3, 1997: Bergoglio is appointed coadjutor archbishop of Buenos Aires.

February 28, 1998: Bergoglio succeeds Cardinal Quarracino as archbishop of the capital of Argentina.

February 21, 2001 Pope John Paul II names Bergoglio a cardinal.

2003: Congress votes in favor of nullifying the law of "dutiful obedience" that protected those responsible for crimes committed during the dictatorship from going to trial. The president of Argentina is Néstor Kirchner, a neo-peronist and a member of the left wing of the Justicialist Party.

2005: Bergoglio is elected president of the Episcopal Conference of Argentina. He is re-confirmed in 2008.

April 18, 2005: Bergoglio participates in the papal conclave in Rome electing Benedict XVI. According to reliable sources, he finished second.

June 14, 2005: The Supreme Court definitively nullifies the laws of "dutiful obedience" and the "end point," re-opening the doors to pursuing "judicial truth."

April 25, 2007: The Federal Criminal Court declares the pardon—granted in 1990 by President Menem to Jorge Rafael Videla and Emilio Eduardo Massera—unconstitutional. Their 1985 sentences of life imprisonment remain valid.

November 8, 2010: Admiral Massera dies at 85 while interned in a military hospital, never having recovered from a brain aneurysm of 2004.

November 8, 2010: Bergoglio is questioned during the "ESMA trial."

December 22, 2010: Videla is once again sentenced to life in prison for the death of thirty-one inmates.

July 5, 2012: Videla receives a new sentence of fifty years in prison for abduction and theft of identity committed to the children of the desaparecidos.

March 13, 2013: Bergoglio is elected pope choosing the name of Francis. He is the first bishop of Rome to name himself after the saint of Assisi.

May 17, 2013: Videla dies in prison at the age of 87.

BIBLIOGRAPHY

BERGOGLIO, J.M., Papa Francesco. Il nuovo papa si racconta, Conversazione con S. Rubin e F. Ambrogetti, Salani, 2013.

BERGOGLIO, J.M. – SKORKA, A., Il cielo e la terra. Il pensiero di papa Francesco sulla famiglia, la fede e la missione della Chiesa nel XXI secolo, a cura di D.F. Rosenberg, Mondadori, 2013.

HIMITIAN, E., Francesco. Il papa della gente. Dall'infanzia all'elezione papale, la vita di Bergoglio nelle parole dei suoi cari, Rizzoli 2013.

Nunca más. Rapporto della Commissione nazionale sulla scom-parsa di persone in Argentina, Emi, 1986.

ROSTI, M., Argentina, Il Mulino, 2011.

VERBITSKY, H., L'isola del silenzio. Il ruolo della Chiesa nella dittatura argentina, Fandango Libri, 2006.

ZANATTA, L., Storia dell'America Latina contemporanea, Later-za, 2010.

ACKNOWLEDGMENTS

POPE Francis had just been elected. I wrote my first article about him after interviewing some of his old friends from Buenos Aires. I had not yet finished the work, when uncertainties regarding the actions of Jorge Mario Bergoglio at the time of the dictatorship already began filling the airwaves.

I did not know much. I spent the night reading, skimming through books and querying Internet search engines. There was much that did not add up. Some documents were controversial, others clearly forged.

The next morning, I sent a text message to Marco Tarquinio, my manager: "If you want, I can work on the accusations against Bergoglio. There are dubious documents and false images circulating." After the editors received it, I received an okay. This led to an investigation published by *Avvenire** in five parts. It was possible that our research could have turned up something controversial or compromising. But we decided to get to the bottom of

---

* A popular lay-run Catholic newspaper in Italy.

it anyway. Therefore, I am grateful to Marco Tarquinio and his intuition.

Of course, this work would not have come about without Stella Sciacca and Lorenzo Galliani. For weeks they accompanied the process, from the initial inquiries in search of confirmations to the drafting of the text. Without their insatiable curiosity, astuteness, patience and determination, *Bergoglio's List* would have been like a table with only three legs.

I am also grateful to the editors of *Avvenire*, who in the days of the "counter inquiry"—while other celebrated media outlets were uncritically embracing Bergoglio's accusers—supported yours truly. Among the many I cannot neglect to mention are Alessandro Zaccuri, for his encouragement and much more; Andrea Lavazza, Luciano Moia, and the chief editors who gave me the first assignment on the new Pope, which led to this work; Lucia Capuzzi (those one who benefited at least once from her observations and her address book know what I mean). And Philip Rizzi—a gracious friend before becoming colleague—a formidable expert of ecclesial affairs and all things "Jesuit."

Many others have contributed as well. Among those who cooperated with our research, I am grateful to the archbishop of Monreale, Msgr. Michele Pennisi, the bishop of Concordia-Pordenone, Msgr. Giuseppe Pellegrini, my colleague, Ms. Silvina Perez, the staff at SERPAJ (Service for Peace and Justice), and the Nobel Peace Prize winner, Adolfo Pérez Esquivel.

Thanks also go to the Argentine journalists (a real wealth of information), who do not give up despite ostracism from powers that be in Buenos Aires.

Insofar as unusual, I cannot exempt myself from expressing gratitude to the publisher who accepted my proposal and put the best available experts and resources necessary to compile "Bergoglio's List."

I also owe a closing farewell to all those who slammed the door in my face, who kept their mouths shut, and to those who advised me to "Let it be." They also deserved this book.

SAINT BENEDICT✝PRESS

Saint Benedict Press publishes books, Bibles, and multimedia that explore and defend the Catholic intellectual tradition. Our mission is to present the truths of the Catholic faith in an attractive and accessible manner.

Founded in 2006, our name pays homage to the guiding influence of the Rule of Saint Benedict and the Benedictine monks of Belmont Abbey, just a short distance from our headquarters in Charlotte, NC.

Saint Benedict Press publishes under several imprints. Our TAN Books imprint (TANBooks.com), publishes over 500 titles in theology, spirituality, devotions, Church doctrine, history, and the Lives of the Saints. Our Catholic Courses imprint (CatholicCourses.com) publishes audio and video lectures from the world's best professors in Theology, Philosophy, Scripture, Literature and more.

For a free catalog, visit us online at
SaintBenedictPress.com

Or call us toll-free at
(800) 437-5876